THE LEGACY OF SLAVERY IN BRITAIN

Nigel Sadler

AMBERLEY

The author would like to dedicate this book to the memory of all those who suffered the indignity and horrors of being enslaved and to those who fought against this injustice.

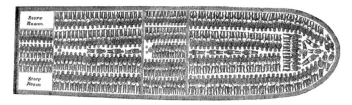

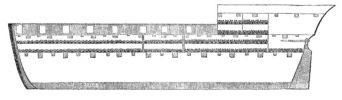

One of the lasting images of the transatlantic slave trade is that of the slave ship *Brookes* laden with a cargo of Africans. The illustration was created by Thomas Clarkson (his monument is on page 18) in 1787, depicting the *Brookes* with 454 humans packed into the hold for the journey from Africa to Jamaica. It was one of the first propaganda illustrations that in a simple form depicted the root of the argument in a political campaign and was a pivotal tool in gaining the abolition of the British slave trade in 1807. This image is often the inspiration for illustrations used in many subsequent campaigns and is regularly used in publications that cover the transatlantic slave trade. It is possible to argue that the campaigns for the abolition of the slave trade (1807) and the abolition of slavery (1834) have been used as models for many campaigns since.

First published 2018

Amberley Publishing
The Hill, Stroud
Gloucestershire, GL5 4EP

www.amberley-books.com

Copyright © Nigel Sadler, 2018

The right of Nigel Sadler to be identified as the Author
of this work has been asserted in accordance with the
Copyrights, Designs and Patents Act 1988.

British Library Cataloguing in Publication Data.
A catalogue record for this book is available from the British Library.

ISBN 978 1 4456 8013 2 (print)
ISBN 978 1 4456 8014 9 (ebook)

Typesetting and Origination by Amberley Publishing.
Printed in Great Britain.

Contents

	Introduction	5
Chapter 1	Monuments and Memorials – Hero or Villain?	15
Chapter 2	Houses	38
Chapter 3	City Landscapes – What's in a Name?	47
Chapter 4	Industrial and Commercial Landscapes	69
Chapter 5	Collectables	81
Chapter 6	Racism	85
Chapter 7	The United Kingdom Overseas Territories	90
	Acknowledgements	95
	Bibliography	96

Copper ingots known as manillas were shipped to Africa to trade for human cargo. These were made in many parts of the UK, such as Exeter and Birmingham. Samples of these can be found in many museums in the UK; for example, moulds for manillas are on display in the Royal Albert Memorial Museum in Exeter. Museums and archives throughout Britain hold many items that tell the story of enslavement and emancipation, which are often hidden away in their stores. (Author's Collection, on display at Vestry House Museum, 2007)

Introduction

One of the most deplorable chapters in British history was the complicit involvement of the government, the ruling classes and big business in the transatlantic slave trade and the use of enslaved labour to build individual and national wealth. Many in Britain know little of the extent of British involvement in the transatlantic slave trade or how all around them today is the legacy of the wealth made through slavery or signs of the struggle against the trade and for abolition.

The transatlantic slave trade developed around a triangular route. Goods made in Britain were carried down to Africa and traded for captive Africans. Between 1500 and 1888, between 12 and 16 million Africans were captured and transported against their will to the Americas. It is estimated that a similar number were killed in the process of collecting these people and while waiting to be boarded onto ships. The ships that had carried the trade items to Africa were then loaded with these captured Africans, who were carried to the Americas. On the crossing, between 10 and 25 per cent died from disease, starvation, suicide and murder by the crew.

Photographed in 2008, Brimstone Hill Fortress, St Kitts, represents the dominance of the British Navy and Army in the West Indies, symbolising Britain's power. It provided a physical means to safeguard British interests in the region, not only against the French and Spanish, but also the enslaved workers living in the British territories. However, often forgotten, it is also a testament to the skills of the enslaved craftsmen and labourers who physically built it.

Above and below: Ruins of Cheshire Hall Plantation, Providenciales, Turks and Caicos Islands, where cotton was produced. It is now a tourist attraction. Below, the author sits in a moment of contemplation at the Cheshire Hall Plantation ruins in 2003.

The survivors were then sold as enslaved labourers. The harsh work, illness, punishment and the brutality of their lives meant that most of the Africans were not expected to survive in the New World for more than ten years, and the African population was expected to help provide new labourers through the birth of the next generation. The ships that had journeyed from Africa were then made ready to be loaded with produce made by the enslaved – i.e. cotton, sugar and tobacco – which was carried on their homeward journey back to the UK.

There are powerful symbols and legacies in both Africa and the Americas. In Africa, the forts built to protect the trade and where the captive Africans were held before being forced onto the ships stand as a sad testament to the evils one man can do to another. These have become places to remember the mostly anonymous Africans who passed through these buildings. In the Americas, especially the Caribbean, the buildings used to control the enslaved labour, and those that processed the sugar, cotton, tobacco and other produce stand as ruins or are still used in the production of these items today. The homes of plantation owners stand as a monument to the wealth created for a few through the blood, sweat and tears of the enslaved workers. There are also government buildings, churches and boundary fences, which were often built using enslaved labour and are still being used today for the same purposes, ignoring the fact of whose hands and skills built some of the present infrastructure of community and civic life. Some have also been turned into hotels, and market the fact of their plantation history.

While there are structures in the Caribbean such as plantation houses, civic buildings and boundary walls and locations that record the struggle for their freedom, these types of sites are not present in Britain. While slavery was legal in its empire, it remained illegal in Britain, and up until recently it was felt that such legacies to the transatlantic slave trade did not exist in the United Kingdom. However, the trade has left a physical and psychological mark. There are monuments to philanthropists who made their wealth through slavery, houses built from the profits made through trading in Africans and the use of enslaved labour to produce items such as sugar and cotton, and many city landscapes bear the names of those who were involved or who profited from it.

These connections have become more apparent and have been promoted, or questioned, because of two recent bicentenaries: first, the anniversary of the 1804 independence of Haiti in 2004, which created the first country to be governed by formerly enslaved people; and secondly, the bicentenary of the abolition of the British Slave Trade in 2007. This second anniversary saw £20 million made available through the Heritage Lottery Fund to carry out commemorations in the UK. The year saw the opening of the International Slavery Museum in Liverpool as well as plethora of major exhibitions such as 'Breaking the Chains' at the British Empire and Commonwealth Museum in Bristol, 'Sugar and Slavery' in the Museum of London Docklands and 'The Royal Navy and the Slave Trade' in the Royal Navy Museum in Portsmouth. There were also a range of much smaller exhibitions in community museums such as 'Enfield and the Transatlantic Slave Trade' at Forty Hall, which used items from its collection such as sugar bowls, cotton clothing and hard wood furniture to explain how the materials used in these items could have been produced by enslaved labour. These exhibitions provided some temporary understanding of the transatlantic slave trade and its legacy, but in many cases, rather than being the start of further exploration, they were the end product and the next local or national commemoration/celebration theme became the priority.

These exhibitions and the story of the transatlantic slave trade becoming part of the national curriculum has encouraged a new generation of young eager minds to start to question. This has been supported by organisations like the National Trust and Historic England carrying out more detailed research on their properties and collections and making this information available online or as part of the interpretation the public are given during a tour. This has seen many reinterpretations of buildings and museum collections to tell a new story, sometimes from the view of the enslaved rather than the enslaver or the person profiting from their labour. New plaques were erected to honour formerly enslaved people living and campaigning in Britain, while the role of women in the abolition movement was also explored in more detail, but more importantly it illustrated how engrained the legacy of slavery is in the British landscape.

Many of Britain's major towns and cities illustrate the complexities of the slave trade through their public spaces, mainly in the statues depicting nearly always white men who helped to finance and/or build their town/city or who were local dignitaries. Many people wouldn't take a second look at statues depicting sixteenth to mid-nineteenth-century people, but these monuments depict their good deeds while ignoring their less worthy actions, often including some involvement in the trade in enslaved Africans, with produce created through enslaved labour and the profits made from financing such ventures or by their outspoken support of the slave trade.

Old debates have been renewed about the suitability of those honoured with statues in towns and cities. Abolitionists like William Wilberforce and Thomas Clarkson are not questioned, but benefactors and businessmen like Edward Colston in Bristol (see page 33) and Robert Millington (see page 34) in London are disputed as their legacy might have benefited their city, but it was done using money and profits secured through the slave trade or the use of enslaved labour. National heroes like Sir Francis Drake and Lord Horatio Nelson have also been drawn into this debate. Their military achievements are clear, but it is their involvement with, or support of, slavery that questions the single-story dialogue these statues represent and promote.

Sometimes the link to slavery is unknown to the local population, or has transcended from its original slavery association to a new, more important social link. A good case is Penny Lane in Liverpool, named after James Penny, a Liverpool slave trader, in recognition of his philanthropic work in the town. In 2006 there was a suggestion that his link to slavery meant that his name being used on a street was inappropriate. However, a stronger campaign won the day as the street was the inspiration for the Beatles song 'Penny Lane', released in 1967, and Beatles fans were unwilling to see this cultural link to the Fab Four being lost.

Some of these towns and cities have embraced the complicated and controversial history behind their development and growth. They have tried to address some of the issues, especially since 2007, sometimes being local government-led, but often driven by community concerns. Now the history in these cities is not hidden and is open for debate and to be redressed. However, other cities, like Plymouth, are still disconnected from their slavery past, though even here there now appears to be a plan to provide some recognition in the city by 2020.

For many it is hard to associate modern morals and ethical behaviour with actions carried out in the past by the government and some well-respected individuals; this was another time, where other realities existed, no matter how much we wished they didn't. Should well-known landmarks be removed and hidden? What would London, for example, be without Nelson's Column? What would Plymouth call its main shopping centre? It shouldn't be a matter of trying to eradicate the better known narrative by removing it to replace it with a lesser known narrative; what good would this do in creating a greater understanding of the past? We need to acknowledge what happened, note how it is being recorded and to correct the biases that we now see around us in our modern towns and cities and in things that many hold dear.

Some organisations have actively researched how their buildings and collections were created to identify ties to either emancipation or the involvement and profiteering from the trade in enslaved workers or produce made by them. At the same time, it isn't about asking for an individual's connection to the slave trade being recorded or mentioned at every point they are portrayed. Why would it be necessary to highlight Nelson's pro-slavery connections on board HMS *Victory* moored in Portsmouth, which is in effect a memorial to the Battle of Trafalgar? However, at key places such as at Nelson's Column in Piccadilly Circus, it is essential to try and give a balanced viewpoint of the perceived good and perceived bad of an individual because at these venues it is an issue of national identity, or in the case of Edward Colston's statue in Bristol, of a regional identity.

Individual and Personal Links

Many people in Britain have strong religious beliefs, but they might not know how their chosen religion played a part in both maintaining slavery and fighting for emancipation. The Catholic Church used the Bible to condone slavery by citing that the New Testament taught slaves to obey their masters. It is argued that this did not accept slavery, but it is clear that some Catholic clergy and even Popes owned enslaved Africans. While some Popes did issue Papal Bulls forbidding slavery, these were often ignored by the Catholic royal courts in Spain and Portugal. The Anglican Church wasn't any better. It was the nonconformist religions, especially the Wesleyans (Methodists) and the Quakers, who fought long and hard to end slavery.

While it is easy to see the buildings, read the street names and research the statues, there are some legacies either ignored or not explored. On the simplest level, the British have a love affair with sugar. Much of the sugar used today is made from sugar beet rather than sugar cane. However, our sweet tooth stems from the fact that through enslaved labour, sugar as a cheap commodity was a reality and became a staple part of our diet. It is therefore no surprise that one of the most successful actions to try to end slavery was the sugar boycott of the late 1700s.

Another link is surnames. A good example is chef and TV personality Ainsley Harriott, who searched for his ancestry during the programme *Who Do You Think You Are?* The BBC programme aired in 2008 showed not only the complexities of ancestral links, but also the fact that many Caribbean people could trace their family lines not only to the enslaved, but also to the plantation owners, those who owned enslaved labour. Ainsley Harriott's great-great grandfather was James Gordon Harriott, a white slave owner, who had a relationship with one of his enslaved labourers. It is uncertain if this was a consensual relationship or not, but it resulted in the birth of Ebenezer, Ainsley's great-grandfather. Ebenezer was born a slave, so he would have legally become the property of James Gordon Harriott, as well as his son. Like many people who are descended from African-Caribbean lineage, they carry a lasting legacy of the days of enslavement – their surnames. They inherited their surname through a blood tie, like Ainsley Harriott, or were assigned their former slave master's surname either during enslavement, or more likely just after emancipation. For some, this was too big a burden to carry. In America, one of the most high profile name changes was Cassius Clay, who did not want to have any tie to his ancestral family's slave owner, from whom they had inherited their surname. He became Muhammad Ali, and stated 'Cassius Clay is a slave name. I didn't choose it and I don't want it. I am Muhammad Ali, a free name – it means Beloved of God, and I insist people use it when people speak to me'.

Some groups were clearly persecuted in Britain, but often based on religious beliefs rather than colour of skin, including anti-Catholicism, anti-Semitism and the persecution of Huguenots. However, it was not until the slave trade that colour became a major issue, leading to the most significant and destructive legacy of slavery – racism (pages 85-89). To make slavery 'acceptable', Africans were dehumanised, and this was done through both colour and their lack of Christian beliefs – it was easy to marginalise a group of people if you did not understand them, their beliefs or their differences.

Unfortunately, the arguments surrounding the legacy of slavery are complicated. Some people argue from emotion, others from a political viewpoint, while others argue to defend those who are no longer here to defend themselves. It is easy to say that we cannot and/or shouldn't impose our moral and ethical modern views on events that happened in a time where different laws and different norms were accepted. We shouldn't try and replace one history with another, no matter how well meaning the intention. History shows us that people we consider as 'good' carried out some despicable things, which at the time were neither illegal nor immoral to the social norms of the day. For us to judge by today's standards can be seen as harsh. Therefore, shouldn't we look at correcting the biases in our history and the way history is represented around us, rather than eradicate one part of history that we don't like in an attempt to sanitise the past to make the modern citizens feel better about themselves?

We are all the legacy of transatlantic slavery. Our ancestors included enslavers, the enslaved, the people who consumed produce made by enslaved labour, or whom manufactured goods to be exchanged and shipped to Africa and to the Americas to be used on the plantations, and those that fought against slavery. It is just a matter of the degree of our knowledge of these ancestors and our willingness to accept the realty of the transatlantic slave trade, how it invaded everyone's life and how we all live with that legacy. Rather than trying to correct past wrongs, we should be looking to educate, remember and commemorate the past, but it is our actions today in how we address modern slavery and the purchasing power we as the consumer have to make sure slave labour is not used to make the goods we buy today that is probably more relevant.

Hopefully this book will inspire people to go out and start to explore the street names and buildings that surround them. Many cities now have formal and informal tours that take visitors to sites linked to slavery and emancipation. These tours often surprise the people taking them with how popular and well-known buildings fit into the story. You never know, your local links to the story of slavery may be closer than you think.

People on a 'slavery tour' of London, May 2008.

A Brief Overview of Slavery

To put some stories included in this book into context, a short overview of Britain's involvement in the transatlantic slave trade and the development of and profit from the production of crops by enslaved labour is included below.

1562 – John Hawkins departs Plymouth on his first journey to pick up captured Africans to trade them in the Americas. This is viewed as the first involvement by the English in the transatlantic slave trade.

1600s – Britain develops its empire in the Americas, seeing land being claimed especially in North America and the Caribbean. These new lands needed to be developed economically and a plantation economy was encouraged. This required a large amount of labour, which was met through the importation of enslaved Africans.

1772 – The public became fascinated with the James Somersett case. He was an escaped slave recaptured in England and placed on a ship bound for the West Indies. Granville Sharp defended him and Chief Justice Lord Mansfield ruled that no man could be a slave in Britain. This clarified the position that no-one could be a slave in this country, so any enslaved workers arriving on these shores were effectively freed, becoming domestic servants to their former owners. However, if they returned to the Americas and Caribbean, their position of enslavement returned as well.

1781 – The captain of the slave ship *Zong* threw 133 captive Africans overboard to their death, claiming it was a necessary loss due to the lack of food and water. He claimed £30 compensation for each lost African from the insurers, as he would have done for any other form of livestock. In 1783, at a hearing in the London Guildhall (page 72) Chief Justice Lord Mansfield ruled compensation did not have to be paid as the captain and crew were at fault, but also refused to view the killings as murder. The British public became horrified when learning of the cruelty faced by Africans onboard the slave ships, leading to many abolition groups being set up.

1783 – While dining with his friend Gerard Edwards, Wilberforce met Reverend James Ramsay, a ship's surgeon who had become a clergyman on the island of St Christopher (later St Kitts) in the Caribbean, and a medical supervisor of the plantations there. The conditions endured by the slaves, both at sea and on the plantations witnessed by Ramsay, horrified him. When Ramsey returned to England after fifteen years in the Caribbean, he met Sir Charles Middleton, Lady Middleton, Thomas Clarkson, Hannah More and others, who later became known as the Testonites, a group interested in promoting Christianity and moral improvement in Britain and overseas. They were appalled by Ramsay's reports of the depraved lifestyles of slave owners, the cruel treatment meted out to the enslaved and the lack of Christian instruction provided to the slaves. With their encouragement and help, Ramsay spent three years writing *An Essay on the Treatment and Conversion of African Slaves in the British Sugar Colonies*, which was highly critical of slavery in the West Indies. Published in 1784, it raised public awareness and interest, but led to West Indian planters attacking both Ramsay and his ideas in a series of pro-slavery tracts.

1787 – Meetings with Thomas Clarkson, Granville Sharp, Hannah More and Charles Middleton led to Wilberforce championing the parliamentary campaign for abolition of the slave trade. The Society for Effecting the Abolition of the Slave Trade formed, bringing Quakers and Anglicans together in the same organisation for the first time. The committee chose to campaign against the slave trade rather than slavery, as members believed slavery would disappear as a natural consequence of the abolition of the trade. The campaign was the world's first grassroots human rights campaign, in which men and women from different social classes and backgrounds volunteered to try to end the injustices suffered by others.

1788 – Parliament passed law regulating the number of slaves allowed per ship. The fight for emancipation was male dominated but women wanted to become more involved publicly. Hannah More urged a friend 'to taboo the use of West Indian sugar in your tea' and at La Belle Assemblée, a concert hall in Brewer Street, Soho, London, 'ladies were permitted to speak in veils'.

1788 – More than 100 petitions were sent to parliament in support of the cause. Manchester alone furnished 10,639 signatures.

1789 – On 12 May, William Wilberforce made his first major speech on the subject of abolition in the House of Commons.

1791 – Wilberforce, though involved informally, officially joined the committee of Society for Effecting the Abolition of the Slave Trade.

1791 – The first Parliamentary Bill to abolish the slave trade was easily defeated. The government were able to prohibit insurance companies from reimbursing ship owners when slaves were thrown overboard.

1792 – A debate at the Coachmakers Hall, Foster Lane, Cheapside, called for the boycott of West Indian sugar and rum. The motion was carried by a unanimous vote of 600. This was led by women, who were denied political power but could influence the economy. Women, as chief purchasers of household goods, were encouraged to boycott slave-produced sugar from the West Indies, and in 1792 the sugar boycott affected as many as 300,000 people. Women also purchased sugar bowls bearing anti-slavery messages. Instead, they used East India sugar, which was produced by free labour.

1792 – 519 petitions were submitted in support of Wilberforce's proposed abolition Bill. Manchester (with a population of 75,000) produced 20,000 signatures.

1792 – The popular campaign collapsed because of the French Revolution and the slave uprising in modern-day Haiti. The public at this point were more concerned about a similar fate befalling Britain.

1792 – A free colony was established in Sierra Leone to bring together black settlers from Britain and freed enslaved Africans to live and work equally with white settlers. The British Government assumed responsibility for the colony in 1808. Wilberforce and Granville Sharp were involved in this.

1793 – A vote to abolish the slave trade was narrowly defeated.

1795 – The Society for Effecting the Abolition of the Slave Trade ceased to meet. Wilberforce continued to introduce abolition bills throughout the 1790s. When Napoleon reintroduced slavery in the French colonies, support of abolition was no longer perceived as being pro-French.

1804 – The Society for Effecting the Abolition of the Slave Trade began meeting again, and Wilberforce's Bill to abolish the slave trade successfully passed all its stages through the House of Commons. Its reintroduction during the 1805 session, however, was defeated.

1806 – The Foreign Slave Trade Bill received Royal Assent on 23 May 1806. This Bill banned British subjects from aiding or participating in the slave trade to the French colonies, which in effect abolished the British slave trade. It was the result of parliamentary manoeuvrings, rather than public disputes.

1807 – The Slave Trade Act received Royal Assent on 25 March 1807. Other countries did not follow suit, and some British ships continued to operate illegally. The US abolished the slave trade in 1808, and Wilberforce lobbied the American Government to enforce its own prohibition more strongly. Oddly, the overall transatlantic slave trade increased following the end of the British slave trade.

1817 – The compulsory registration of the enslaved, together with details of their country of origin, became law. This became the Slave Register, which was kept for each country.

1819 – The Royal Navy formed the Anti-Slavery Squadron. Unfortunately, the well-meaning anti-slavery patrols and anti-slavery action ended up having ulterior motives. There was the developing trade demands from Britain and then the expansion of the British Empire into Africa. In 1861 the area around Lagos was brought under the control of the British, claiming it was necessary to stamp out slavery, but in reality it was to get a foothold for colonial expansion.

1821 – Thomas Fowell Buxton took over leadership of the abolition campaign in the House of Commons.

1823 – The Society for the Mitigation and Gradual Abolition of Slavery (later the Anti-Slavery Society) was formed, arguing that emancipation was morally and ethically required, and that slavery was a national crime.

1824 – Wilberforce made his last anti-slavery speech in parliament.

1832 – The Reform Act of 1832 brought more abolitionist MPs into parliament.

1833 – Wilberforce made his final anti-slavery speech at a public meeting in Maidstone, Kent.

1833 – In May, the Bill for the Abolition of Slavery was presented. Wilberforce heard that the Bill was passed by the House of Commons and he died in July. In August, the House of Lords passed the Slavery Abolition Act.

1834 – In August, the Abolition Act became law in most of the British Empire. Nearly 800,000 enslaved workers were freed, the vast majority in the Caribbean. Plantations owners started to be paid their allotted compensation for the loss of their enslaved workers, and in total the government agreed to compensation totalling £20 million. This accounted for about 40 per cent of the Treasury's expenditure that year. None of the money went to the enslaved and they gained no access to land. To provide a new source of cheap labour, plantation owners turned to bringing in indentured labour from India.

1834- A six-year apprenticeship scheme was introduced so that all former enslaved workers over the age of six in the Caribbean could 'learn' how to be good free citizens. In reality, it extended the period of cheap labour for the plantation owners.

1838 – The apprenticeship scheme ended two years early because of protests in the UK, and the apparent ineffectiveness of it.

1867 – Following abolition of the slave trade in Cuba, the British African Squadron is withdrawn.

This timeline presents the formal view of the major legal and political changes that brought around emancipation. In reality, it is a one sided view. It is wrong to believe that emancipation was brought about by the British citizens and government; after all, if the system had remained economically profitable, it probably would have continued for a much longer period. What made it uneconomic was war and conflict in Europe making it harder to maintain protected trade routes, but more importantly the enslaved were seeking their own freedom through civil disobedience. Uprisings occurred throughout the Caribbean from the earliest days but had become more costly and violent. There were uprisings in Antigua (1735), Barbados (1675, 1692 and 1816), Demerara (1823) and Jamaica (1742, 1745 and 1831). In the latter country the conflict had become so costly in the eighteenth century the British Government provided land to some escaped enslaved workers, known as Maroons, to bring about some peace, and giving them some degree of autonomy. However, it was an uprising in a French colony that scared the political leaders. The 1791 Revolt in Haiti eventually led to Haiti's independence in 1804, with the loss of around 5,000 French soldiers. The British feared the loss of face if something similar happened in one of their territories.

Images Used in this Book

The book uses a range of Victorian prints, early twentieth-century postcards and twenty-first-century photographs taken by the author. This mix is intended not only to provide the reader with a range of illustration types, but also to show the breadth of images created throughout nearly 200 years of history since the abolition of slavery in 1834. The postcards come from the heyday of postcard manufacturing and collecting, less than a century after Britain outlawed slavery in its territories. This period falls at the mid-point between today and the abolition of the slave trade (1807) and of slavery (1834). They are just distant enough from slavery that no one who knew slavery would be alive, yet at a time when the injustices of the slave trade and holding humans in slavery was not really thought about or in most cases considered worth addressing. This means these postcards are from a time when the street names and statues had been established with no concerns about what they represented. It was not until the twenty-first century that questions started to be asked about the public realm of towns and cities and what story it was really telling about the place and its development. These postcards show some street scenes long gone, others now modified and some where little has changed over the last century. They have been chosen because somewhere in them is a link to slavery or emancipation, often forgotten but now being questioned.

The towns and cities covered, along with the stories, are taken as examples of the types of legacies that one can find. Similarities will apply to many houses, streets, towns and cities throughout Britain.

Chapter 1

Monuments and Memorials – Hero or Villain?

Britain's landscape is scattered with monuments and memorials to many organisations and individuals. When one starts to look at monuments that have any connection to the transatlantic slave trade, many of these are to people, nearly all white men, but they recognise other aspects of their life rather than their connection to slavery or emancipation. It is easy for some towns to embrace their links to people who were involved in the anti-slavery movement. However, others recognise a person's importance in other areas, often overlooking their links to, or support of, enslavement, the slave trade and profiting from the labour of enslaved workers. It is time that the duality of many people's lives are recognised and addressed more publicly. For example, some people, like Francis Drake or Lord Nelson, are national heroes and for many their actions in warfare outweigh all their other actions. For others, nothing could forgive a person's role, no matter how small, in forcing Africans into slavery or profiting from their misery, pain and even death.

Abolitionists and the Abolition Cause

William Wilberforce

William Wilberforce (1759–1833) became an independent MP for Kingston on Hull in 1780, aged just twenty-one, able to support either Whig or Tory policies depending on which he agreed with. He became an independent Member of Parliament for Yorkshire (1784–1812) and in

William Wilberforce.

Above: Wilberforce Monument, Hull, *c.* 1910.

Below left: Wilberforce, as featured in the *London Illustrated News* on 22 October 1859. The image comes from an unfinished portrait by Sir Thomas Lawrence in 1828.

Below right: Wilberforce Monument, Hull, *c.* 1910.

1785 his concern for reform started when he became an evangelical Christian. His deep-seated religious convictions led to a career campaigning for the importance of religion, education and morality. It was a meeting with Thomas Clarkson, Granville Sharp, Hannah More and Charles Middleton in 1787 that led to him championing the parliamentary campaign for the abolition of the slave trade. Following the success of the end of the British slave trade in 1807, he became involved in the campaign for the complete abolition of slavery, which he continued even after his political career ended in 1826 due to ill health. He died just three days after hearing that the Act would be passed through parliament. He was buried in Westminster Abbey, close to his friend William Pitt the Younger. A seated statue of Wilberforce by Samuel Joseph was erected in 1840.

In 1834 a public subscription in Hull funded the Wilberforce Monument, a 31-metre (102-foot) Doric column topped by a statue of Wilberforce. The monument was erected at Whitefriargate, near Prince's Dock, with the foundation stone being laid on 1 August 1834 – the day slavery in the British colonies was officially abolished. When the Queen's Dock closed in the 1930s, it was moved to the eastern end of Queen's Gardens, where it towers over the forecourt of Hull College.

Thomas Clarkson

Thomas Clarkson was a leading campaigner against the slave trade. It could be argued that he, not Wilberforce, was the person whose actions led to the abolition of the slave trade in 1807. While the campaign needed a political leader to lobby the politicians and push the arguments in Whitehall, there also needed to be people to gather the data that would make their arguments stronger.

As a founder member of the Society for Effecting the Abolition of the Slave Trade, his enthusiasm to end slavery started as a student in Cambridge. Reading widely on the subject, he was introduced to other leading anti-slavery campaigners, such as Granville Sharp. Collecting data was dangerous, however, and during a visit to Liverpool a gang of

Thomas Clarkson.

Clarkson Memorial, Wisbech. Postmarked 1934, this postcard was sent a century after the British abolition of slavery.

sailors were paid to assassinate him, but their attack failed to kill him. He gathered together the instruments of slavery and punishment – handcuffs, shackles, thumbscrews and branding irons – to illustrate the barbaric nature of the trade, having realised that objects and pictures illustrated the issue better than any written word. It was Clarkson who acquired the plans for the slave ship *Brookes* (page 2) that became the iconic anti-slavery image. Following the abolition of the slave trade in 1807, Clarkson continued to lobby the end of slavery, not just in Britain but internationally. There are various memorials to Clarkson. In 1857, an obelisk commemorating Clarkson was erected in St Mary's churchyard. In 1879, a monument was erected in Wadesmill at the spot he resolved to devote himself to the abolition of slavery, and the Clarkson Memorial was erected in his birthplace of Wisbech. In 1996, a tablet was dedicated to Clarkson's memory in Westminster Abbey, located near the tomb of William Wilberforce.

Josiah Wedgwood
A member of the Darwin–Wedgwood family, and the grandfather of Charles and Emma Darwin, for many, Josiah Wedgwood's fame comes from his very collectable pottery. However, he also played a major part in the anti-slavery movement, joining the organising committee of the Society for the Abolition of the Slave Trade (formed in 1787). He asked one of his craftsmen to create a seal to stamp in the wax used to seal envelopes used by the committee. This image, a kneeling chained African with the words 'Am I Not a Man And a Brother?', became used in every conceivable item, and was probably the first logo designed for a political cause. This image became a symbol not only for the British anti-slavery campaign, but also the American campaign. Men displayed the image on shirt pins and buttons, whereas women used the image on adornments such as bracelets, brooches and hairpins. While women were denied the vote, they politicised this logo and women started to use a similar image but depicting a woman and the words 'Am I Not a Woman And a Sister?' Many argue

Josiah Wedgewood.

Inauguration of Josiah
Wedgewood's statue,
Stoke-on-Trent,
in 1863, from the
*Illustrated London
News*

An American version from 1858 of Josiah
Wedgewood's iconic kneeling enslaved man.

that the iconic kneeling enslaved male/female begging for their freedom was not a correct perception of reality: many were not subserviently asking for their freedom, but rather were actively fighting for it. The statue of Josiah Wedgwood (1730–1795) holding a replica of the Portland Vase at Winton Square, Stoke, was paid for by public subscription and was created by sculptor Edward Davies. A second bronze was cast from the original mould in 1957 and this statue was erected outside the Wedgwood Visitor Centre.

Even though it is Josiah Wedgwood we all remember, there was a family tradition of fighting against slavery. In 1764, Sarah Wedgwood (1734–1815) married her third cousin, Josiah Wedgwood. She brought with her a considerable dowry, which came under Wedgwood's control. Sarah helped Josiah with his work, recording his experiments, keeping accounts and giving practical advice on shapes and decoration, and she also supported his anti-slavery work. Josiah and Sarah had seven children. One of these was Sarah Wedgewood Junior, who in 1825 joined with Lucy Townsend, Elizabeth Heyrick, Mary Lloyd and Sophia Sturge to form the Birmingham Ladies Society for the Relief of Negro Slaves (later becoming the Female Society for Birmingham). The group was a leading part of the sugar boycott, actively targeting not only shops selling sugar, but also the purchasers of sugar, often the lady of the household. They visited homes, distributing pamphlets and organised public meetings to get their message across, often gathering together petitions calling to end enslavement. This society inspired other independent

Above left: Grey's Memorial, Newcastle upon Tyne, *c.* 1909.

Above right: Thomas Paine's statue in Thetford, 2015.

female groups to form and by 1831 there were seventy-three women-only anti-slavery groups. Sarah Wedgwood Junior died in 1856, and neither of the Sarah Wedgwoods have been honoured with a statue to remember their work.

Charles Grey

Some monuments to people who played a significant role in abolition carry no mention of this action. Charles Grey, 2nd Earl Grey, became Prime Minister in 1830 and his tenure saw two major changes in law: the Reform Act of 1832 and the Abolition of Slavery in 1833 (becoming law in 1834). His monument in Newcastle upon Tyne was made by Edward Hodges Bailey, the creator of Nelson's Column in Trafalgar Square. Grey's column contains a staircase and a viewing platform at the top, and the plaque on the monument records:

> This column was erected in 1838 to commemorate the services rendered to his country by Charles Earl Grey K. G. who, during an active political career of nearly half a century was the constant advocate of peace and the fearless and consistent champion of civil and religious liberty. He first directed his efforts to the amendment of the representation of the people in 1792, and was the minister by whose advice, and under whose guidance, the great measure of parliamentary reform was after an arduous and protracted struggle safely and triumphantly achieved in the year 1832.

The Abolition Act became law in 1834 but was followed by a six-year apprenticeship scheme, so full abolition had not been achieved when the monument was constructed. It might be for this reason that abolition was not included as one of his achievements.

Thomas Paine

In the late 1700s there were a number of people who would cross paths, whether it was fighting for general rights for people or the liberation of the enslaved. One of these was Thomas Paine (1737–1809), who has a statue in his home town of Thetford, Norfolk. He was a political activist and revolutionary, becoming one of the founding fathers of the United States, where he emigrated to in 1774. He was also involved in the French Revolution and lived in France for most of the 1790s. His most famous publication was *The Rights of Man*, published in 1791. This collection of articles argues that all human rights are granted by nature and therefore not at the whim of governments or individuals. He said that individuals could take up arms to gain their freedom. Even though not directly involved in the anti-slavery movement, his works inspired some to fight for the rights of the enslaved. See the Spence Token on page 81, which illustrates his influence.

Charles James Fox

Charles James Fox (1749–1806) was the arch rival of William Pitt the Younger. His father, Henry, a leading Whig of his day, had similarly been the great rival of Pitt's famous father. He was an eloquent orator and could forcefully make his point. His politics challenged the establishment, especially during the American War of Independence, which he supported as he saw George III as a tyrant. He was forced out of government by the king in 1782 and served most of the rest of his political career in opposition. He became a vocal anti-slavery campaigner and supported France during the Revolutionary War.

Erected in 1816, the bronze figure, created by Richard Westmacott the Younger, holds a copy of the Magna Carta in his right hand and sits upon on a granite pedestal. It is thought that he is depicted seated as this was more flattering, due to him being a large man. There is also a statue of him in St Stephens Hall, Westminster, where he stands among other famous parliamentarians.

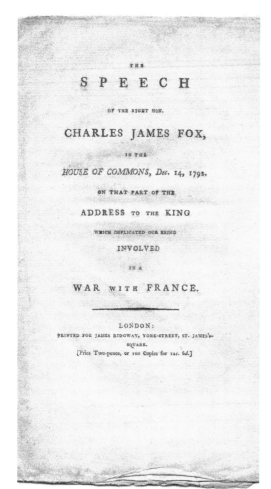

Above: An engraving of the statue of Charles James Fox, Bloomsbury Square Gardens, London, published in 1817.

Left: The cover of a public speech given by Charles James Fox in 1792 regarding the possibility of becoming involved in a war with France.

Prince Albert

One of the causes that Prince Albert (1819–1861) took to heart was the abolition of slavery around the world. Against advice, he took up an active position in the anti-slavery movement, and as President of the African Civilisation Society for the Extinction of the Slave Trade he gave a speech at the anti-slavery meeting held at Exeter Hall, 1 June 1840 (page 48). In his speech he stated:

> I have been induced to preside at the meeting of this Society from a conviction of its paramount importance to the great interests of humanity and justice. I deeply regret that the benevolent and persevering exertions of England to abolish that atrocious traffic in human beings (at one the desolation of African and the blackest stain upon civilised Europe) have not as yet led to any satisfactory conclusion.

This was Prince Albert's first public speech after he had married Queen Victoria in February 1840. His presence increased demand for tickets and this was the first time that the abolitionist movement had gained Royal approval. His support, and the reception his speech received, increased the anti-slavery sentiment among all classes.

The Albert Memorial, London, 2007.

John Wesley

John Wesley (1703–1791) established the Methodist Church as he felt the Anglican Church failed to call sinners to repent, that it was corrupt and that God had called him to bring about a revival in the Church. A statue of John Wesley on horseback was erected in 1932 at the chapel he established in 1739 as the first Methodist meeting room in the world (page 66). Wesley was based in Bristol for much of the 1740s and 1750s.

He was an avid abolitionist, speaking out and writing against the slave trade. He published a pamphlet on slavery in 1774, entitled 'Thoughts Upon Slavery', in which he wrote: 'Liberty is the right of every human creature, as soon as he breathes the vital air; and no human law can deprive him of that right which he derives from the law of nature.' He influenced George Whitefield to journey to the colonies, spurring the transatlantic debate on slavery, and missionaries travelled throughout the British West Indies preaching to the enslaved.

Wesley, a friend of other abolitionists like John Newton and William Wilberforce, is remembered in a variety of statues/busts such as at Lincoln College, where he was elected as a fellow in 1726, teaching Greek and lecturing on the New Testament as he continued his own studies.

John Wesley's bust, Lincoln College, Oxford, *c.* 1920

Above: John Wesley's statue, City Road, London, *c.* 1920.

Left: John Wesley on horseback in the courtyard in front of Wesley's new room (Chapel), Bristol, *c.* 1935.

Matthew Boulton

Matthew Boulton was one of the eighteenth century's greatest entrepreneurs. He acquired the lease of the Soho Mill in 1761 and developed it into Soho Manufactory. He expanded the cottage next to it into Soho House, moving into it when the Manufactory was completed.

MATTHEW BOULTON.
BORN, 1728
DIED, 1809.

Matthew Boulton.

In 1789, Samuel Wyatt was commissioned to extend the buildings and revamp the gardens. On Boulton's death, the house passed to his son Matthew. Soho House is now a museum celebrating Matthew Boulton's life, his partnership with James Watt, his membership of the Lunar Society and his contribution to the Midlands Enlightenment and the Industrial Revolution. It was the home of entrepreneur Matthew Boulton from 1766 until his death in 1809, and a regular meeting-place of the Lunar Society of Birmingham.

In Birmingham city centre there is a gilded bronze statue showing Matthew Boulton, James Watt and William Murdoch by William Bloye and Raymond Forbes-Kings. It was funded through a £8,000 bequest from Richard Wheatley in 1939, and £7,500 from the city council. Using preliminary designs drawn up in 1938 it was unveiled in 1956 on a Portland stone plinth on Broad Street, Birmingham. Due to its colour it is locally known as 'The Golden Boys' or 'The Carpet Salesmen' due to the rolled up plan of a steam engine they are examining. The statue was restored and re-gilded, and replaced in its old position in September 2006. The statue was removed in 2017 in preparation for its transfer to the Centenary Square.

Boulton and Watt improved and developed the steam engine. These engines not only industrialised the UK but were also exported to the plantations in the Caribbean to replace wind and horse-power. It can be argued that this was a positive move as the plantations now needed fewer enslaved workers. Boulton was an abolitionist, but many iron manufacturers in the Midlands objected to the abolition campaign because their businesses relied on the trade to Africa for slaves both in trade items and the equipment for imprisoning the enslaved, shackles for example, and with the slave plantations. In the end, the abolition of the slave trade and slavery did not undermine local iron industries. Soho Museum is an impressive link between Atlantic slavery and the early English metal industry, which supplied the equipment for the slave ships, and exports to Africa and the plantations.

Abraham Lincoln
It isn't just British people represented in statues in Britain. A replica of the statue of President Lincoln in Lincoln Park, Chicago, was unveiled by Prince Arthur, Duke of Connaught, after being ceremonially presented by the American ambassador and accepted by Prime Minister David Lloyd George. Initially the statue was to be erected in 1914, but was postponed. By that

Statue of Abraham Lincoln, President of the United States 1861–1865, in Parliament Square, London, 2007.

time some favoured an alternative statue by George Grey Barnard, which was eventually erected in Manchester. Lincoln was the leader of the Union Army during the American Civil War, a war fought over the individual states' rights for self-determination, including the issue of slave ownership. Lincoln is seen as the emancipator of the enslaved in the USA.

Anti-Slavery Memorials
The Archway, Stroud

There are a few monuments that reflect the anti-slavery movement. One of the best known is the Archway, which stands on the corner of the Paganhill Estate in Stroud. It is the only memorial of its type in Britain and was built to celebrate the abolition of slavery in the British Colonies. In 1833, Henry Wyatt (1793–1847) purchased Farmhill Park. In 1834 he laid out a new carriageway from Farmhill Lane to the house and the entrance he created at this point commemorates his association to the Stroud Anti-Slavery Society. The inscription chosen by Wyatt reads:

ERECTED TO COMMEMORATE THE ABOLITION OF SLAVERY IN THE BRITISH COLONIES THE FIRST OF AUGUST, A.D. MDCCCXXXIV

The Archway was threatened with demolition in 1958 when the estate was sold, but was saved and restored in 1960–61 and again in 2000. Its grand purpose as a main entrance to an estate is now gone, and it stands with terraced houses along a busy road.

There is a lasting legacy for the Archway. In 1962, Archway School opened on part of the old Farmhill Park. In recent years the pupils have raised funds for a UN campaign to end contemporary forms of slavery and they have attended conferences in Geneva promoting the worldwide UNESCO project 'Breaking the Silence', which aimed to reveal the truths behind the transatlantic slave trade.

Considering the significance of the abolition Acts, it is surprising that the Archway is probably the only significant memorial to the Act rather than to individuals involved. More surprisingly, it was not until the new millennium that monuments appeared that honour the enslaved themselves. In 2005 the 'Captured Africans' sculpture was unveiled on St Georges Quay, Lancaster, as a memorial to the enslaved Africans transported on ships originating out of Lancaster. The City of London Memorial to the Abolition of the Slave Trade at Fen Court, unveiled in 2008 by Archbishop Desmond Tutu, commemorated the 2007 bicentenary of the Act to Abolish the Transatlantic Slave Trade. Created by Michael Visocchi, it consists of columns in the form of sugar cane placed around a podium, suggesting a pulpit and a slave auction.

The anti-slavery memorial arch in Stroud, *c.* 1910.

Westminster Abbey, with
St Margaret's Church on the
left, London, *c*. 1910.

Westminster Abbey

Many churches contain memorials to local dignitaries, some of whom were either famed abolitionists or made their wealth through slavery. Wilberforce was buried in Westminster Abbey next to his friend William Pitt the Younger. His memorial statue, by Samuel Joseph (1791–1850), was erected in 1840 in the north choir aisle. Other abolitionists are also commemorated in the abbey.

Thomas Fowell Buxton

Thomas Fowell Buxton was an abolitionist, social reformer and the MP for Weymouth for nineteen years. He married Hannah Gurney, whose sister was Elizabeth Fry, the reformer.

At a time when clean drinking water was of concern in London, Thomas Fowell Buxton's son, Charles Buxton, erected a memorial drinking fountain to commemorate his father's role in the emancipation of enslaved workers throughout the British Empire in 1834. Completed in 1866, the memorial, designed in collaboration with the neo-Gothic architect Samuel Sanders Teulon (1812–1873), also commemorates fellow abolitionists William Wilberforce, Thomas Clarkson, Thomas Babington Macaulay, Henry Brougham and Stephen Lushington. The illustration shows the memorial in its original location in Parliament Square.

The Buxton Memorial Drinking Fountain, *Illustrated London News*, 1879.

ERECTED IN 1835
BY
CHARLES BUXTON M.P.
IN COMMEMORATION OF
THE EMANCIPATION OF SLAVES 1834
AND IN MEMORY OF HIS FATHER
SIR T. FOWELL BUXTON
AND THOSE ASSOCIATED WITH HIM
WILBERFORCE, CLARKSON, MACAULAY, BROUGHAM
Dᴿ LUSHINGTON AND OTHERS

The Buxton Memorial in Victoria Tower Gardens, 2008.

It was removed from the square in 1949 as part of the post-war redesign and it was not re-erected in Victoria Tower Gardens until 1957.

In 1989 an additional memorial plaque was added to commemorate the 150th anniversary of the Anti-Slavery Society and a major restoration programme was undertaken as part of the commemoration of the 200th anniversary of the act to abolish the slave trade in 2007. The original inscription on the fountain reads:

Intended as a memorial of those Members of Parliament who, with Mr. Wilberforce, advocated the abolition of the British slave trade, achieved in 1807; and of those members of Parliament who, with Sir T. Fowell Buxton, advocated the emancipation of the slaves throughout the British dominions, achieved in 1834. It was designed and built by Mr Charles Buxton, MP, in 1865, the year of the final extinction of the slave trade and of the abolition of slavery in the United States.

Olaudah Equiano

Olaudah Equiano was born in Africa and was enslaved at the age of eleven. His given slave name was Gustavus Vassa. One of his masters, Captain Pascal, permitted his baptism in St Margaret's Church, Westminster. He was educated by British sailors and on his voyages was able to privately trade, making enough money to buy his freedom in 1768. Olaudah Equiano worked in Plymouth to help ex-slaves get to Sierra Leone in 1787.

Following a stint as a hairdresser in London, he returned to sea on various expeditions, even seeing polar bears in the Arctic. He played a significant role in the campaign to end the British slave trade, but died in 1797 before seeing it enacted. He married Susanna Cullen in 1792 and had two daughters, Ann Maria and Joanna (page 68).

While white men of power were commemorated with statues and memorials soon after they died, other emancipationists have long been forgotten, and their deeds go unremembered. However, Olaudah Equiano was a major player in the struggle for slave rights and it is therefore shocking to learn that it took until 2000 for the city of Westminster to unveil a plaque at 67-73 Riding House Street, which reads:

Olaudah Equiano (1745–1797), 'The African', lived and published here in 1789 his autobiography on suffering the barbarity of slavery, which paved the way for its abolition.

Above: Olaudah Equiano.

Right: The plaque for Olaudah Equiano at St Margaret's Church, Westminster.

His place of burial is not known. Therefore, to honour him other moments in his life have been identified as places to recognise him. In 2009, the Archbishop of York unveiled a plaque by sculptor Marcia Bennett-Male near the font in St Margaret's Church, Westminster, where Equiano was baptised when he was still a slave. The inscription reads:

'THE AFRICAN' OLAUDAH EQUIANO
BAPTIZED GUSTAVUS VASSA
In this church 9 February 1759
Author & Abolitionist

For many, these plaques are insufficient considering his role, and the fact that he had been enslaved and was an African. It often raises the question of why there isn't a statue of him.

Hannah More

Hannah More (1745–1833) was a poet and writer that lobbied for social reform. She became well known for her writings on abolition and encouraging women to become involved in the anti-slavery movement.

There is an impressive but simple bronze plaque in William Street, Bath, marking the fact that Hannah More lived there from 1792 to 1802. The homes of many women such as Hannah More served as meeting places for all-women groups simply because such meetings were often deemed unsuitable in public houses and municipal spaces.

Left: Hannah More, *c*. 1830.

Below: All Saints' Church in Wrington, North Somerset, *c*. 1910.

ALL SAINTS CHURCH & GRAVE OF HANNAH MORE WRINGTON 281

Hannah More is buried in the graveyard of All Saints' Church, Wrington. Unlike her male contemporaries, Hannah More is not given the honour of a statue in a public square or prominent location. Her only memorial is her headstone in the churchyard and her bust, opposite one of John Locke (the father of Liberalism), which stand on either side of the entrance door. There is also a wall monument to Hannah More, dated 1833, above the south door.

Pro-Slavery or Beneficiaries of Slavery

When it comes to statues of people who were pro-slavery, they will never state this ideological view on the plinth. Instead, the statues recognise the good deeds done by that person. These statues range from those who are now little known up to national monuments of people we would class as National Heroes. This, therefore, raises the question of whether we are able to distinguish and honour the person's positive achievements without also acknowledging that they were not perfect. Or, should their statues be removed, as some campaigners suggest?

Admiral Lord Nelson

Watching over London atop his column, which was erected between 1840 and 1843, is Admiral Lord Nelson (1758–1805). Voted number 9 in the 100 Great Britons in the 2002 BBC poll, his heroics during the Napoleonic Wars are legendary. However, his pro-slavery stance is less well known. Nelson's wife, Frances, was born in Nevis and owned an enslaved worker called Cato. The Nelsons were married on the Montpelier Estate in Nevis, a sugar plantation utilising enslaved labour. Nelson was also stationed in the Caribbean, where his role as a Navy officer was to enforce British rights, including protecting the slave trade and the exportation of trade produce made by enslaved labour. Nelson wrote a scathing attack on Wilberforce, feeling that his actions would undermine the British Empire, especially in the West Indies colonies. In a letter dated 10 June 1805 to Simon Taylor, a Jamaican plantation owner that Nelson had befriended when stationed there thirty years earlier, he stated that he had to 'launch my voice against the damnable and cursed doctrine of Wilberforce and his hypocritical allies'. This letter was read out to parliament.

His link to slavery and the colonial past has raised a great deal of debate in Barbados, where there have been calls for his statue, erected twenty-seven years earlier than the one in London, in the former Trafalgar Square to be moved as it is no longer fitting to the renamed area, now known as National Heroes Square.

In 2017, a storm erupted when journalist Afua Hirsch raised the question about the suitability of Nelson's Column in London. She gained support but also a lot of opposition, while another journalist, Max Hastings, called it 'silly nonsense'. It illustrated the extreme ends of the spectrum either to keep or removal with no middle ground, no compromises offered. In 2018, Afua Hirsch presented the television programme *The Battle for Britain's Heroes* about the issue of sanitised British history, including the statues of Nelson and Colston. However, she did suggest a compromise through the reinterpretation of the statues, leaving them in situ and promoting better education through teaching all aspects of our colonial past.

In 2010, the Forth Plinth in Trafalgar Square became the temporary home for Yinka Shonibare's 'Nelson's Ship in a Bottle'. Its aim was not only to celebrate the success of Nelson at the Battle of Trafalgar, but also the postcolonial multi-cultural Britain that Nelson's Column stands in. Many saw it also reflecting the fact that Nelson's victory was aided by black sailors on HMS *Victory* and other Navy ships.

Above: Yinka Shonibare's 'Nelson's Ship in a Bottle', 2010.

Left and below: Nelson's Column, London, *c*. 1910.

Edward Colston

Edward Colston (1636–1721) was born in Bristol, where he became a merchant and Member of Parliament. He used his wealth for philanthropic purposes such as building schools and alms-houses and supporting several churches along with the hospital. For all of this good work he did for Bristol a statue designed by John Cassidy was erected in his honour in 1895. However, this statue has become the centre of a bitter campaign as it fails to recognise that his philanthropic work to help the underprivileged in Bristol was at the cost of Africans.

In 1680, Colston became a member of the Royal African Company, which controlled a monopoly in slave trading. He rose to the position of deputy governor, its most senior executive position, in 1689. His transactions became more personal when in 1684 he became a partner in a sugar refinery in St Kitts, which used enslaved labour.

Above left and right: The plaque and statue in 2007, with red paint placed on his name by a protestor, depicting the blood of enslaved africans.

Right: Stereoscope of the Colston Memorial, Bristol, *c*. 1910.

In 2014, a Bristol newspaper reported that 56 per cent of the respondents wanted the statue to remain, and 44 per cent wanted it to be removed. Interestingly, a middle ground appears to have been reached and the statue is to remain, but a new plaque will be attached to it detailing his links to the African slave trade and how he made his money. Therefore, rather than hiding the statue away, this will encourage debate and allow a more balanced view of this man and his conflicted past.

Robert Milligan

Robert Milligan (1746–1809) grew up on his family's Jamaican sugar plantation. He left in 1779 and established himself as a businessman in London, but maintained his links to slavery. At his time of death he owned 526 enslaved workers on his two Jamaican sugar plantations. He was the driving force behind the development of the West India Docks in London (page 74).

Robert Milligan's statue was commissioned in the year of his death, 1809, by the West India Dock Company, employing sculptor Richard Westmacott to carry out the work. The statue stood at its present location from 1809 until 1875, when it was moved to the main gate, where it stood until 1943. It was then held in storage before being erected at the London Docks. It was returned to its original position in 1997 by the London Docklands Development Corporation.

Statue of Robert Milligan, West India Docks, outside the Museum of London Docklands, 2010.

Francis Drake

A statue by Joseph Boehm was erected in 1884 to commemorate Drake's circumnavigation of the globe in 1580. As Drake proudly stares out to sea from Plymouth Hoe, the memorial records his exploits. It, however, conveniently leaves off one of Drake's historic 'achievements' – his involvement in the earliest English journeys transporting enslaved Africans to the New World.

Sir Francis Drake's statue on Plymouth Hoe is a replica of the one in Tavistock. Drake was born just outside of Tavistock at Crowndale Farm, which has since been demolished. The studio model for this statue can be seen at Buckland Abbey.

Plymouth has embraced Sir Francis Drake as a National Hero for his role in defeating the Spanish Armada in 1588 and in his role as an explorer. Drake Circus shopping centre opened in 2006 (page 64) and proudly displays his name for all to see. However, the town is not so

Sir Francis Drake's
memorial in
Plymouth, postmarked
March 1905.

Drake Memorial, Plymouth.

211

Sir Francis Drake's memorial on Plymouth Road, Tavistock, postmarked 1953.

willing to highlight that some of his first journeys as a captain were to take enslaved people from Africa to Hispaniola. It is interesting to note that the Tavistock Town Council records that 'in 1567 Drake and Hawkins sailed out of Plymouth on a slave-trading voyage to the West Indies and first tangled with the Spaniards'.

John Hawkins

John Hawkins is believed to have been England's first slave trader. He left the Barbican (page 76) in Plymouth in 1562 with three ships. In Guinea he seized 400 Africans, transporting them across the Atlantic to be traded like animals in the West Indies. With his cousin Francis Drake, Hawkins made three such journeys between 1562 and 1567, seizing in total around 1,400 Africans. It is estimated that the capture and transportation of these Africans could have resulted in the death of an equal or greater number of Africans.

At this time Hawkins would have been helped in his kidnapping of the majority of these Africans by other Africans. Not only did this trade make him personally wealthy, but it also raised his status within the court of Queen Elizabeth I, with him becoming Treasurer for the Navy in 1577 and being knighted in 1588 following the defeat of the Spanish Armada.

Hawkins appears not to have ended his slave trading by choice. In 1567, his ships encountered the Spanish, and in the ensuing fight many of his men died. In total he lost 325 men on his final voyage, but it was still very profitable.

In Plymouth there are places that recognise John Hawkins and mark his achievements, including Sir John Hawkins Square. Even though the city has publicly remembered John Hawkins as 'England's first slave trader', there is no monument or sign recording this or recognising the inhumanity he showed to the Africans he kidnapped.

Right: Sir John Hawkins.

Below: Sir John Hawkins Square, Plymouth, 2018.

Chapter 2

Houses

Throughout Britain there are a number of houses that were owned by those fighting for emancipation of the enslaved. However, there are more numerous houses that link to people who were involved with the slave trade, profited from slavery or from the produce created by enslaved labour; indeed, far too many to include in this publication. However, what is included is a cross section of these connections and how the houses either address or ignore their links.

Buckland Abbey
Originally founded as a Cistercian abbey in 1278, Buckland Abbey remained an abbey until Henry VIII's Dissolution of the Monasteries. In 1541, Sir Richard Grenville the Elder started to convert the building into a house. His grandson Richard Grenville completed the conversion in 1575–76. Unusually, the church was the main part of the site that was converted into the house, while the remainder of the site was demolished.

Richard and Francis Drake despised each other and it was for that reason that Drake purchased the house through intermediaries in 1581, so that Richard wouldn't find out that it was he who wanted the house. Drake lived in the house for fifteen years and his descendants remained there until 1946. The print below dates from 1829, when Britain still allowed the legal ownership of enslaved workers in its West Indian colonies. It is probable that the owner was at least utilising produce created by enslaved labour.

In 1946 Arthur Rodd purchased the site and presented the property to the National Trust in 1948. The National Trust website records that the house was 'sold again to privateer Sir Francis Drake, the first Englishman to circumnavigate the globe'. There is no mention of his link to the slave trade.

Buckland Abbey, seen in a print from 1829.

Buckland Abbey,
c. 1910.

Buckland Abbey,
c. 1905.

Wilberforce House

Wilberforce House, a former merchant's house with access to the River Hull, is the birthplace of William Wilberforce (1759–1833), famed for his involvement in the successful campaigns to abolish the slave trade (1807) and slavery (1833), which became his life work as a Member of Parliament. The house became a museum in 1906 and benefited from a £1.6 million redevelopment as part of the bicentenary of the Abolition of the Slave Trade in 2007. The exhibitions in the museum give an insight into Wilberforce, the anti-slavery movement and West African culture.

Oriel Chambers is next-door to the museum and is the home of the University of Hull's Wilberforce Institute for the Study of Slavery and Emancipation, which conducts research into historic and contemporary forms of slavery and was established in 2006.

Fishponds

Hannah More's father was a schoolmaster who had originally pursued a career in the Church of England. He set up his own schoolhouse in Fishponds, where Hannah was taught, and she went on to help set up schools to encourage education for all. In the 1790s Hannah wrote material covering moral, religious and political topics, including slavery, which was mainly distributed to the literate poor.

Wilberforce House, Hull, *c.* 1910.

Statue of William Wilberforce outside Wilberforce House in Hull, his birthplace, seen *c.* 1910.

The cottage in Fishponds, near Bristol, where Hannah More was born.

Penrhyn Castle

The original fortified house built in the fifteenth century was reconstructed in the 1780s, but what is there today was created between 1822 and 1837. It was designed by Thomas Hopper for George Hay Dawkins-Pennant, who had inherited the estate from his second cousin, Richard Pennant. The construction of the Norman revival building is estimated to have cost the equivalent of between £40 and 50 million in today's money. The Pennant family made their fortune from the sugar industry and slave plantations in the Caribbean, and family members set up trading interests from Liverpool. The profits from their various business enterprises revolving around slavery was invested in the estate, including an art collection, and into local slate quarries.

The Georgian House

The Georgian House was opened as a museum to John Pinney (1740–1818), its owner. However, in the mid-2000s the museum shifted its focus and started to pay more attention to Pinney's servant, Pero Jones. Today, the museum website states that: 'The house was built in 1790 for John Pinney, slave plantation owner and sugar merchant. It was also where the enslaved man of African descent, Pero Jones, lived.'

Along with an adult, twelve-year-old Pero and his sisters, Nancy and Sheeba, were purchased in Nevis by plantation owner Pinney in 1765. When the Pinney family moved from Nevis to England in 1783, Pero and the freed slave Frances Coker moved with them. Pero was John Pinney's servant and Frances was Jane Pinney's lady maid. The family moved to Bristol in 1784, with John becoming one of the wealthiest men in the town. Frances and Pero visited Nevis in 1790, and Pero visited again in 1794. It is unknown why this last visit changed Pero, but on his return he started to drink regularly and his behaviour became unacceptable. When he fell ill in 1798 he was sent to the country with the hope fresh air would improve him and the Pinney family visited him. Sadly, he died, aged about forty-five. He was never formally given his freedom, so he lived and died as an enslaved person, having been in the ownership of the Pinneys for thirty-two years.

There is a memorial to John Pinney in St Michael and All Angels' Church, Somerton. In March 1999, a new footbridge across the River Frome in Bristol harbour was named after Pero, to commemorate one of the enslaved who lived and died in the city.

Penrhyn Castle,
Llandygai, Bangor,
c. 1905.

The Georgian House Museum, 7 Great George Street, Bristol, 2007.

Clandon Park

Thomas Onslow (1679–1740), 2nd Baron Onslow, rebuilt Clandon Park in 1733. He married Elizabeth Knight, the daughter of a Jamaican merchant, and through her inherited the 2,000-acre Whitehall Plantation, on which enslaved labour grew sugar cane. Profits from the sale of this sugar built and maintained the house from its construction in 1733 until the abolition of slavery in 1834. Onslow was also a leading figure in the Royal Exchange Assurance Corporation, which had dealings in the slave trade.

Thomas Onslow (1754–1827), 2nd Earl of Onslow, inherited Clandon Park and it is believed that he voted against the abolition of the slave trade in 1796.

The house was gifted to the National Trust in 1956 and was extensively restored. However, the surrounding park was kept in private ownership of the Onslow family. In April 2015, the house was gutted by a fire and much of the collection held in the house was lost. Even though the National Trust has done a lot to address the issue of hidden histories in their properties, dealing with subjects like the connections of houses and families to slavery, the fire at Clandon House raised a debate over whether the property should be restored at a cost of £30 million. The restoration had already been criticised by the family of the ancestral owners, who said that whatever was rebuilt would be a copy.

In March 2017, Pete Grieg, leader of the 24-7 Prayer movement, criticised the National Trust's plans, stating that this was restoring a property that had been built from the profits of the slave trade. In response a spokesperson for the National Trust stated that the cost of the rebuilding would be met by the insurance money, which could not be spent on anything else, and that the National Trust had a legal and moral obligation to preserve buildings entrusted to its care, stating:

We recognise that Clandon was built partly with money inherited from Elizabeth Knight's uncle, who profited from the slave trade. We have never shied away from acknowledging this aspect of

Clandon's history and our research is ongoing. When considering interpretation for Clandon in the future, we will continue to explore its links to the slave trade and other important aspects from its 300-year-old history.

Raleigh House

Even small towns have connections to emancipation and slavery. Opposite the Methodist Church in Ottery St Mary is Raleigh House. This house was built in 1805 and the owner, Thomas Davy, along with his sister Rebecca, inherited Topsham Plantation in Jamaica from their brother Edward, who had set it up just before dying in 1803. Thomas and Rebecca never visited the plantation and their other brother, James, took on responsibility of running Topsham Plantation, as well as his own nearby plantation. They appear to have been the archetypal absentee slave owner. The 1817 slave register shows that all the slaves aged over fourteen had been born in Africa and had probably been transported to Jamaica in about 1803, where they were purchased by Edward.

Within these towns there are also connections to the abolition movement. Letters exist that indicate that the community lobbied to end slavery. A petition signed by around eighty Ottery St Mary men (there are no signatures from women) was sent to the king in 1814, asking for Anglo-French peace not to include permission for the French to restore their slave trade. This was just one of 861 petitions, with a total of 755,000 signatures being gained,

Clandon House, Surrey, *c.* 1910.

Raleigh House (left) stands opposite the Methodist Church (page 67) in Ottery St Mary, Devon, *c.* 1900.

Raleigh House, seen in 2018.

and the sheer scale of opposition led Prime Minister Castlereagh to raise the priority of international abolition, which led to the French agreeing to abolition in 1815. Even though a prominent resident and doctor in the town, Thomas Davy did not sign the petition from Ottery St Mary, probably because as a slave owner he could not be seen to be supporting any attempt to protect the rights of the enslaved.

Harewood House
The home of Edwin Lascelles (1713–1795), Harewood House was built between 1759 and 1771. It was designed by architect John Carr, who utilised the finest craftsmen in its construction, with the interior being designed by Robert Adam. Inside, many furnishings were made by Thomas Chippendale, while outside Lancelot 'Capability' Brown created the gardens. Portraits of family members were painted by Reynolds, Gainsborough, Lawrence and Richmond. This house was only possible because Henry Lascelles, who died in 1753, left a fortune, estimated to be worth around £28 million today. This fortune had been created because the family were merchants trading from London and Bristol to Barbados, and who had also been customs collectors in Barbados. They lent money to planters, and when debts remained unpaid they took over the plantations and all assets, including enslaved workers.

By the time of emancipation they owned property in Barbados and Jamaica, as well as on a few other Caribbean islands, and received £26,000 in compensation for the loss of 1,277 enslaved workers. Through wise investment the family moved up the British class system to be landed gentry – all built on the back of the suffering of enslaved labour in the Caribbean.

Buckingham House
Buckingham House was built as the townhouse for the Duke of Buckingham in 1703. In 1761, King George III acquired it to become a private residence for Queen Charlotte, at which point it became known as the Queen's House. It was during the Georgian era that Britain dominated the slave trade and King George III did nothing to ease the suffering of the enslaved. He and his household would have benefitted from crops grown by enslaved workers: sugar, cotton, tobacco.

In 1837, Queen Victoria came to the throne, and Buckingham Palace became the London residence of the British monarch. She lived there her with her husband, Prince Albert, who was a staunch anti-slavery lobbyist.

The Rear of Harewood
House, near Leeds,
c. 1910.

Front of Harewood
House, *c.* 1910.

Buckingham Palace,
2009.

Aston Hall

George Austin, born in 1710, went to Carolina in North America and created several tobacco plantations, naming one Shifnal Plantation after his birthplace, and became one of the wealthiest men in the colonies. In 1762, he returned to England with one of his sons, and two enslaved workers, and purchased Aston Hall. George Austin's daughter, Eleanor, stayed in Carolina and married John Moultrie, who owned land and enslaved labour. They moved to Florida in 1764 where he became Lieutenant-Governor of Florida. When Florida returned to Spanish ownership he sold his slaves to the Bahamas and returned to England in 1784. Eleanor inherited Aston Hall and left it to her eldest son, while her second eldest inherited the largest tobacco estate in Carolina, which had been owned by George Austin. There is a memorial tablet at St Andrew's Church, Shifnal, to John Moultrie.

Fonthill Abbey

In 1771, aged just ten, William Thomas Beckford (1760–1844) inherited £1 million (equivalent to around £85 million in 2018) when his father died, the profits of the ownership of plantations that used enslaved labour. The Gothic revival country house was built between 1796 and 1813 by Beckford, with no expense being spared. Beckford lived in the Abbey until he lost two of his Jamaican sugar plantations in a legal case and was forced to sell the house and its contents in 1822. The house was built badly and in haste and much of it was demolished in 1845. The four remaining lodges at the former estate's entrances are a sign of the past grandeur of the site.

Aston Hall, Shifnal, Shropshire, *c.* 1910.

One of the Fonthill Abbey lodges at Fonthill Gifford, Wiltshire, England *c.* 1910.

Chapter 3

City Landscapes – What's in a Name?

Within cities and towns there are many well-known buildings that are connected to the period of slavery but don't advertise the fact. As we travel we follow street names and use buildings as locations. However, how often do we ask who the people these venues and streets are named after or if there was any connection to enslavement?

Kettering

Sometimes it is not the buildings in a city that offers a clue to slavery. Kettering's coat of arms features a black man with a broken chain dangling from his wrist, symbolising the abolitionist work carried out by Reverend William Knibb (1803–1845), who had been born in the town. Knibb was a Baptist minister and missionary to Jamaica, who campaigned against enslavement, once stating:

> The cursed blast of slavery has, like a pestilence, withered almost every moral bloom. I know not how any person can feel a union with such a monster, such a child of hell. I feel a burning hatred against it and look upon it as one of the most odious monsters that ever disgraced the earth. The iron hand of oppression daily endeavours to keep the slaves in the ignorance to which it has reduced them.

In 1988, on the 150th anniversary of the abolition of slavery in the British Empire, he was posthumously awarded the Jamaican Order of Merit, becoming the first white man to receive this honour.

An undated badge showing the Kettering coat of arms.

Exeter Hall

The anti-slavery movement in Britain didn't end with the Emancipation Act of 1834, as it soon developed into supporting the freedom of all enslaved workers. In 1840, English Quaker Joseph Sturge organised the World Anti-Slavery Congress in London to unify anti-slavery groups in the UK and USA. The meeting, which took place during 12–23 June 1840, was held in Exeter Hall, the Strand, London, and this momentous occasion was captured in a painting by Benjamin Robert Haydon, which hangs in the National Portrait Gallery after being gifted to them in 1880 by the British and Foreign Anti-Slavery Society. It depicts over 130 of the leading anti-slavery campaigners in detail. As mentioned previously, Prince Albert gave a speech at this meeting (page 22).

The Society for the Abolition of the Slave Trade was mainly a Quaker society founded by Thomas Clarkson. When the fight in Britain had been won, the British and Foreign Anti-Slavery Society was founded in 1839. Their mission was: 'The universal extinction of slavery and the slave trade and the protection of the rights and interests of the enfranchised population in the British possessions and of all persons captured as slaves.' In 1990, this group became Anti-Slavery International.

Sometimes it is the location of an event that is significant rather than the building, so even if the building has long gone, the areas importance should still be recognised. After being sold in 1907, Exeter Hall was demolished and the Strand Palace Hotel was built on the site, opening in 1909. Do guests staying in the hotel know what happened on that site during the nineteenth century? The hotel's website does not have any mention of what happened before the hotel was constructed.

The exterior of Exeter Hall, 1843.

The Anti-Slavery Meeting at Exeter Hall, organised by the British and Foreign Anti-Slavery Society.

Above: The Strand, London, 1842.

Right: The Strand Hotel, London, *c.* 1935.

Colston and Bristol

The Bristol horizon has changed dramatically over the last 150 years, with high rises and concrete now dominating the scene. However, at its heart is the city that was built from the profits of slavery. In some areas you can walk down the same streets visited by those who made vast wealth from the misery of enslaved workers. And throughout the town one man's name stands out – Edward Colston (page 33), a major benefactor and philanthropist for Bristol.

Edward Colston's statue (page 33/34) stands on Colston Avenue, which is still a major thoroughfare in Bristol. There is also a Colston Street, Colston Avenue, Colston Hill, Colston Yard and Colston Road in Bristol.

Opened in 1867, Colston Hall took its name from the school founded on this site by Edward Colston in 1708. Colston had originally established a sugar house to refine sugar brought into Bristol Docks from the Caribbean and the site included thirteen workers' cottages. The Sugar House was converted into Colston Boy's School to educate the poor, which remained here until it moved to Stapleton in 1857. Colston Hall Company demolished the school building and built the concert hall.

In April 2017, the charity running Colston Hall announced that 'Colston' would be dropped from the hall's name when it reopened after refurbishment in 2020. This followed protests and petitions, as well as several performers, such as local Bristol band Massive Attack, refusing to play at the hall while it carried the name of a slave trader. The irony is that, although it bears the name of a slave trader, this building had nothing to do with slavery or slave trade, but inherited the name from its geographical position. The hall has also been a place where people's rights have been fought; for example, a meeting for Women's Suffrage was held here in 1880, the Trades Union Congress was held here in 1898 and the Roll of Honour took place in 1919 for soldiers that had been decorated for their service in the First World War.

Bristol Bridge and High Street, postmarked 1907, with the windows and moon cut out so when a light source is placed behind it becomes a night scene.

Colston Avenue,
Bristol, *c.* 1905.

Colston Hall,
Bristol, *c.* 1910.

The interior of
Colston Hall,
Bristol, *c.* 1910.

The Society of Merchant Venturers

In the nineteenth century, education for the masses was very limited. This led to many institutions being developed by the Church and industrial organisations, the latter mainly to educate people for service in their business. Families with children being educated by these establishments did not really care where the money had come from to set up these institutions.

In 1595, it was recorded that the Society of Merchant Venturers set up a school for the children of mariners, and in 1856 they set up a trade school for boys and to provide a range of day and evening classes for adults, including chemistry, mining and engineering. When the Bristol Trade School expanded the Merchant Venturers supported the project, and in 1885 they became financially responsible for it. A new trade school opened in Unity Street as the Merchant Venturers' School. In 1894, it changed its name to the Merchant Venturers' Technical College. The fire of 1906 provided the opportunity to expand the J and a Faculty of Engineering was provided by the Merchant Engineers.

In 1949, the Society of Merchant Venturers sold the technical college to the Local Authority, becoming the Bristol Polytechnic. Nowadays, it is known as the University of the West of England, or UWE. The Venturers' Trust provide support to eight state maintained schools in Bristol and run the independent day school, Colston's School, in Stapleton, which has been supported by the Society of Merchant Venturers since it was founded in 1710.

Merchant Venturers' Technical College.   H. B. & Son, B.

Destroyed by Fire, Oct. 9th. 1906.

Merchant Venturers' Technical College.

Colston Girls School, Bristol, *c.* 1910.

It is probably best to use the text on their website to state their present position:

> The transatlantic slave trade undoubtedly played a significant role in the growth of Bristol during the eighteenth century. Today, Bristol continues to struggle with its past and with the profile of Edward Colston within the city. It is clear that we must address and acknowledge Bristol's historic connection to the slave trade in a way that is illuminating and meaningful.
>
> While we cannot change the past, we can help to eradicate modern-slavery by educating the young people of Bristol about the abhorrence of slavery, both past and present. The Society of Merchant Venturers continually reviews the curriculum at each of our schools to ensure that students are confident, equipped and prepared for the responsibilities they have as global citizens.
>
> By embracing the history of our city, we can all learn valuable lessons that will enable us to build a strong, fair and united future for Bristol, a city proud of its diversity and inclusivity.
>
> The Society of Merchant Venturers is actively working with leaders across Bristol who share our commitment to improve the quality of life for all. Accurately remembering and appropriately acknowledging Bristol's connection to the slave trade is a discussion we are driving forward with purpose.

The present Colston's Girls' School building opened in 1891. Even though the present building has nothing to do with slavery, its financial structure is heavily linked to individuals and organisations that profited from the practice. It originates from endowments left by Edward Colston and the school is still sponsored by the Society of Merchant Venturers. The school addresses its past and its mottos are: 'We cherish our history but look to the future', and 'Go and do thou likewise'.

The Gallery of Modern Art, Glasgow
The Gallery of Modern Art was opened in 1996 in the Old Royal Exchange. This building had evolved out of the townhouse of William Cunninghame, built in 1778. He made his fortune from the tobacco trade, selling produce made by enslaved labour, and owned over 300 enslaved workers on the family plantations in Jamaica. In 1817, the house was purchased by the Royal Bank of Scotland and then underwent major change between 1827 and 1832, including the Queen Street façade of Corinthian pillars and the large hall at the rear, when it became the Royal Exchange. In 1954 it became a library, and then the Gallery of Modern Art.

This is a good example of how a building funded by money from the transatlantic slave trade and the sale of its produce has been modified beyond recognition. Unfortunately, the Gallery seems to omit the origins of its building on their website.

The Royal Exchange, Glasgow, *c.* 1905.

Glasgow

The Port of Glasgow provided access to the Americas. From the mid-eighteenth century it became a major centre for sugar, rum and tobacco, replacing London as the main import port of tobacco grown by enslaved workers, mostly in the southern states of America, especially Virginia. This developed the city and the 'Tobacco Lords', including Glassford, Buchanan, Ingram and Oswald, left their mark on the city. Many built mansions within the city and developed large estates in the nearby countryside. These traders' names are still present in the street names of the city. For example, John Glassford owned plantations and twenty-one tobacco stores in Virginia and Maryland, running a fleet of ships to move the product.

Ingram Street is named after Archibald Ingram (1699–1770), who started out as a street vendor and managed to rise to a position of importance in the city by becoming a tobacco lord and then Lord Provost of Glasgow in 1762. However, the street is now more famous, not because of whom it was named after, but because of a devastating fire. A gas explosion on the night of 17 August 1909 caused a fire that swept along Ingram Street, destroying the area between Shuttle Street and High Street, mostly warehouses containing wine, spirits, clothing and foodstuffs. It took all night to put the fire out.

Sugar was also an important trade for Glasgow residents the Stirlings or the Cunninghames (whose mansion is now Glasgow's Museum of Modern Art), while James Ewing was a major Glaswegian public figure of the early nineteenth century and owned plantations in Jamaica. Many in Glasgow would have had little concern about slavery as they would have had no direct involvement in it; in a sense, they were detached from the reality of slavery, like many people with modern slavery and the products they produce today. These historic links to sugar plantations are still present in the street names, including of Jamaica Street, Tobago Street and Antigua Street, while Virginia Street reflects the tobacco trade.

As more people became informed about the brutalities of slavery, residents of Glasgow joined the anti-slavery movement. This included several lecturers at Glasgow University, who became leading figures in the local abolition movement, including Francis Hutcheson (Professor of Moral Philosophy in 1730), Adam Smith (Professor of Logic and Moral Philosophy in 1751), and John Millar (Regius Professor of Civil Law in 1761).

In 2017, Dr Nina Baker called for a 'symbolic renaming of selected streets' to coincide with Anti-Slavery Day in October to honour important women from Glasgow's past and

Buchanan Street,
Glasgow, *c.* 1905

The Great Fire
on Ingram Street,
Glasgow, August
1909.

Jamaica Street
corner, Glasgow,
c. 1910.

Jamaica Bridge, Glasgow, *c*. 1905.

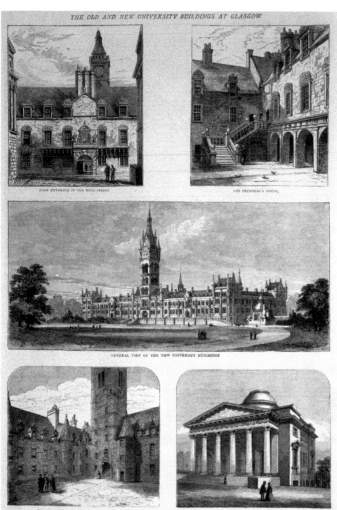

Images of the old and new parts of Glasgow University, from *The Graphic*, 1870.

Glaswegians who campaigned for the abolition of slavery. She was supported by Dr Baker, a Green Party councillor who stated that she thought: 'People are now reasonably aware of the story, but I don't think people walking down these roads will realise the streets are named after these people.'

Manchester
The Industrial Revolution was largely founded on the products of the plantation economies. Manchester's growth was based on cloth production using cotton grown on plantations worked by enslaved labourers. Manchester became home to Henry Brown, an enslaved worker who posted himself in a box from slavery in Virginia to freedom in Philadelphia. Nicknamed 'Box' Brown, he fled the USA to Britain and made a living touring with his exhibition, 'The Mirror of Slavery', and recounting his story of escape. The 1871 census showed he was living in Cheetham Hill and was employing a servant. In 2007, museums across Greater Manchester carried out a 'Revealing Histories' project to identify how the region benefited from slavery.

Hull
Due to its location on the east coast, Hull's maritime trade was mostly with the Baltic and northern Europe. Many would assume the port had no link to slavery, but raw materials were shipped from ports like Hull and were used to trade for enslaved Africans or on West Indian plantations. While Wilberforce fought against slavery, he would have known local people benefitting from the proceeds of slavery.

In 1834, Hull residents John Fisher, Elizabeth Haworth, Thomas Holt, Mary Mills, Thomas Milliken Mills and William Maynard Mills were compensated to free their enslaved labour in the Caribbean. One has to wonder what they thought when passing the Wilberforce Memorial.

Market Street, Manchester, *c.* 1910.

Dock Offices & Wilberforce Monument.   *Hull.*

Hull Dock offices and the Wilberforce Monument, postmarked 1903.

Swansea

Recent research by Chris Evans of the University of Glamorgan has shown that Wales's copper industry helped maintain slavery in Cuba. Welsh industrialists funded the copper mines of El Cobre, near Guantanamo Bay, making them very wealthy and providing Swansea's copper industry with crucial supplies of ore, with ships arriving in Swansea Bay. From a population of 600 in 1827, the population in El Cobre rose to 4,600 by 1841. The sudden demand from Wales in the 1820s saw the mine's owners bringing in slave labour. Cornish miners who had been sent out there were horrified by the treatment of the enslaved workers, who were beaten for even the smallest reason.

Even though slave ownership in British territories ended in 1834, it lasted in Cuba until 1886, despite their slave trade having ended in 1866. The Cuban mine was not closed because of any moral outrage, but because copper prices collapsed.

In this post-emancipation Britain, the Company of Proprietors of the Royal Copper Mines of Cobre's head office was in London and included Mary Glascott and her sons – who owned the Cambrian Works at Llanelli – and solicitor Alexander Druce, a partner in the Llanelly Copperworks Company. Charles Pascoe Grenfell (1790–1867), who would serve as director of the company, was a partner in Pascoe Grenfell & Sons, Swansea's most powerful copper combine. Chris Evans argues that the Grenfells were 'fully fledged Cuban slaveholders', even though Charles Pascoe Grenfell's father had been a friend and supporter of William Wilberforce in his anti-slavery campaign.

The problem with the copper business was that people invested in stocks and these changed hands for large profits, with few people realising what was going on to make the profits that they were benefitting from. Politicians were aware Britons were still benefitting from slavery, however, so in 1843 the Suppression of the Slave Trade Act was passed which

Shewing Free Library in Foreground
and Piers in Distance,
Swansea.

Swansea, *c.* 1910.

forbade any British subject from holding any slaves, even if it was legal to do so in the country in which they were kept.

Swansea wasn't the only place in Wales to benefit from enslaved labour. Anthony Bacon used his profits in the slave trade to back Cyfarthfa Ironworks in Merthyr Tydfil. A second mining operation at El Cobre, the Santiago Company, was headed up by William Thompson, the ironmaster of Merthyr Tydfil's Penydarren Works.

Politics and Slavery

The campaigns for the Abolition of the Slave Trade and Abolition of Slavery could not have succeeded without political support. Without legislation, slavery would have continued, probably until a major revolt by the enslaved. Many debates were held by parliament over a wide number of topics related not only to emancipation, but for the improvement of the welfare of the enslaved. Most notably, debates were held over limiting punishments that could be given, as well as the Slave Registers introduced in 1817, which enabled a full record of the enslaved in British territories to be kept every three years, allowing a greater understanding of the enslaved population – a great help when it came to paying compensation to slave owners in 1834. Even though little remains of the buildings in which these topics were debated, the present Houses of Parliament, built between 1840 and 1876 following a devastating fire, still signify the government that passed the legislation to end slavery, but also of successive governments who have failed to formally apologise for their role in slavery.

As the Empire grew, so did bureaucracy. Officials had to keep in contact with London and this meant that nearly all paperwork was done in duplicate or triplicate. A copy was sent to London, now housed in the National Archives, and ranged from mundane letters to detailed record keeping, recording many aspects of slavery, including original Slave Registers (1817–1834) and the compensation claims as part of the Emancipation Act, creating a legacy of slavery. Private records, especially of plantations, are also found in the libraries of the large estates. Books written during the period of slavery and thousands of books written since 1834 on all aspects of slavery can be found in local libraries, with the largest collection being held by the British Library.

In 1824, the National Gallery opened in the former home of John Julius Angerstein (1732–1823), who had sold his collection of thirty-eight pictures to the government. Angerstein made his money as a Lloyd's underwriter, managing the insurance of slave ships in the Atlantic. He also had a third share in plantations in Grenada, in the Caribbean, and used his wealth to buy artwork and a large home in Pall Mall, later to become the home of the National Gallery.

Palace of Westminster,
London, *c.* 1910.

Palace of Westminster,
London, 2007.

National Archives,
Kew, London, 2002.

Lord Nelson looks down over Trafalgar Square with the National Gallery behind, *c.* 1940.

The complexities of individuals are highlighted by Angerstein. Though a slave owner, he was on the Committee for the Relief of the Black Poor, which had strong abolitionist connections. Even though it moved from Angerstein's former home in 1834, the Gallery's foundations are still tied to money obtained through slavery.

The British Museum is one of many iconic cultural institutions that at first glance have little to do with the legacy of slavery. However, within its walls are collections that relate to both enslavement and emancipation. Opened in 1759, it was based on the collection of Sir Hans Sloane (1660–1753). After studying medicine, Sloane moved to Jamaica, where he married the widow of a plantation owner. From the income from this plantation he amassed a large collection of over 71,000 items at the time of his death.

The postcard overleaf advertises Horniman's tea, a company set up in 1826. It had an indirect link to slavery as people sweetened tea with sugar produced by enslaved labour and it was the sugar boycott that forced the government to take the anti-slavery movement seriously.

Even though it opened in 1759, the British Museum was founded in 1753, and in 2003 the museum recognised this fact by hosting many special events. The museum was wrapped up as if a present to the nation and performances occurred in the galleries, bringing some context to the objects displayed. Over the last twenty-five years or so, the museum has made great strides in addressing the fact that their collection is a symbol of British colonialism, and in part benefitted from some of Britain's negative past, such as its role in slavery.

During the seventeenth, eighteenth and nineteenth centuries, many people involved in slavery gained an education in English universities. Christopher Codrington is a good example. Born in Barbados in 1668, his father was one of the wealthiest sugar plantation owners, as well as being Captain-General of the Leeward Islands. Christopher Codrington was educated at Christ Church College Oxford and became a Fellow of All Souls College. Following a military career, Christopher became Governor-General in the Caribbean and had plantations in Antigua and Barbados. He died in 1710, leaving behind his library of 12,000 books to All Souls College, along with funds to build a library and additional books. The new library building was completed in 1751 and has been used by scholars ever since. It is clear that the funds used for this library (as well as one in Barbados), and those that Codrington used to build up his personal book collection, had come from the profits he made using enslaved labour.

British Museum, London, *c.* 1905.

British Museum in 2003, wrapped as a gift to the nation.

All Souls College, Oxford, 1930s.

Codrington Library, All Souls College, Oxford, *c.* 1910.

Drake Circus, Plymouth, *c.* 1910.

The shopping area original known as Drake Circus miraculously escaped serious damage from the Luftwaffe during the Second World War air raids. It succumbed to development in the 1960s and was demolished in 1966/7, being replaced with a roundabout and a two-level shopping centre. In 2004, it was demolished, with the new shopping centre opening in 2006. Surprisingly, the name of the centre has never been reconsidered, nor has any attempt to address the bias in Drake's history been undertaken.

Between 1834 and 1838, the anti-slavery movement in Birmingham lobbied for change in the apprenticeship scheme, with meetings being held in the town hall, which had opened in 1834. The apprenticeship scheme introduced at the end of slavery in the British territories was in effect a period of transition to benefit the former slave owners, disguised as a period of time during which the emancipated workers would be taught what freedom would mean.

The march was led by an actor dressed as Olaudah Equiano and included a relative of Joseph Sturge, who had led the campaign in Birmingham to end the apprenticeship scheme.

The Society for the Propagation of the Gospel in Foreign Parts, part of the Anglican Church, owned 665 enslaved workers on the Codrington Plantation in Barbados. In 1834, the compensation for these workers was £12,700, the equivalent of over £1 million today, and was paid to Henry Phillpotts, Bishop of Exeter (1830 to 1869), and his colleagues, who used the

Drake Circus Shopping
Centre, Plymouth, 2018.

Birmingham Town Hall,
c. 1900.

An anti-slavery march in
Birmingham, 2007.

Bishops Palace, Exeter, postmarked 1908.

BISHOP'S PALACE, EXETER.

Canterbury Cathedral, 1842.

funds to partially finance the restoration of the Bishop's Palace, Exeter. At the 2006 meeting of the General Synod of the Church of England, delegates voted unanimously to apologise to the descendants of slaves for the church's involvement in the slave trade, while also commemorating their role in helping to pass the Slave Trade Act of 1807.

The Anglican Church had a confused and complicated relationship to slavery. In 1821, a young boy called Adjai was rescued by the Royal Navy, along with other Africans, from a slave ship. Captain Henry Leeke took the Africans to Sierra Leone, where they were freed. Adjai became a Christian and took the name Samuel Crowther and entered the Church in 1843, working with the Church Mission Society. In 1864, he became Africa's first black bishop, and the ceremony took place at Canterbury Cathedral, with Captain Leeke in attendance.

John Wesley (1703–1791) set up the Methodist movement. When his societies needed houses to worship in, Wesley began to provide chapels, first in Bristol at the New Room, then in London (first The Foundery and then Wesley's Chapel) and elsewhere. He was a keen abolitionist, and encouraged those within the Methodist Church to oppose the slave trade. At these chapels, slavery and abolition would have been discussed. The statues that are outside these two buildings are on page 24.

It may appear to be a bit of a stretch, but in effect all Methodist churches could be seen as illustrating the legacy of emancipation. The non-conformist churches led the way in Britain

The doorway to Wesley's Chapel and the preacher's stable, Bristol, *c.* 1920.

Wesley's Chapel, City Road, London, *c.* 1920s.

arguing against slavery, not just at the time of emancipation debate for the British Empire, but throughout many other countries. They also sent missionaries to gather data and to try and make the lives of the enslaved workers easier. One such missionary was Dowson, who travelled through the British West Indies in the early 1800s, trying to preach to informal gatherings of enslaved workers. Methodist chapels both in the UK and the West Indies stand as a testament for the widespread campaign.

The Methodist Church in Ottery St Mary was built in 1829, right at the end of the campaign for the abolition of slavery. There is no evidence that any of the congregation actively fought against slavery, but it is likely that they were aware of the struggle and the position of their church in it. The church is opposite Raleigh House, the home of a slave owner (see page 43/44), showing the complicated association between emancipation and slavery even in a small town.

The Quakers were at the forefront of the abolition movement from its beginnings in 1657. Meeting houses were central in passing on the abolitionist message, so all Quaker meeting houses are part of the legacy of the emancipation struggle. For example, a Quaker congregation was established in Sibford Gower village by 1669, and in 1681 a meeting house was built. The present meeting house replaced the old one in 1865.

Olaudah Equiano's daughter, Joanna (1795–1757), inherited £950 as well as property from her father when she reached the age of twenty-one. Her grave is in Abney Park Cemetery, London. She was mixed race, which wasn't very common in Britain at that time. In 1821 she married the congregational minister, Revd Henry Bromley, at St James, Clerkenwell, an

Anglican parish church in London. He had been ordained a minister at the Independent Chapel in Appledore in Devon, two months prior to the wedding, and he and his new wife lived there for at least five years until they moved to the congregational church at Clavering, Essex. As her father had been enslaved, it is clear that she would have had anti-slavery sympathies, but it is unclear the extent to which she voiced them in this small Devon community.

Above: The Methodist Church, Ottery St Mary, Devon, *c.* 1905.

Right: 'Welcome Words: Or Juvenile Missionary Magazine of the Methodist Free Church', published 1874.

WELCOME WORDS:
OR JUVENILE MISSIONARY MAGAZINE
OF THE
METHODIST FREE CHURCHES.

AFRICANS SEIZED FOR SLAVERY.

MARCH, 1874.   ONE HALFPENNY.

Quaker's meeting house at Sibford Gower, Oxfordshire, *c.* 1910.

Appledore from the air, possibly in the 1930s.

Chapter 4

Industrial and Commercial Landscapes

The British iron industries boomed on the back of slavery, used in the production of chains, padlocks, fetters, the metal used in ship construction (slave ships were sheathed with copper) and the hundreds of thousands of firearms that were shipped to West Africa to exchange for enslaved Africans. In addition, many of the tools used on the slave plantations were manufactured in Britain. For example, Matthew Boulton developed extensive business dealings with the plantations from his factory at Soho in Birmingham.

Unfortunately, the present-day links to organisations that benefited from the transatlantic slave trade are confused because they have diversified their operations, or changed their names. It is interesting to see what major developments happened in the years just prior to slavery being abolished and just after. Many of these developments required large investments of private funds, and it is no surprise to see those that benefited had either made their wealth from selling the produce of enslaved labour, or from the finances procured at the end of slavery through the government compensation scheme.

Often now the site of regeneration, boutique shops and restaurants, many industrial landscapes hide their connection to the slave trade, the support given to the plantation owners through supplying equipment and as an initial destination in the UK to goods made by the enslaved labourers. These are also the points of entry for many of the enslaved domestic servants who arrived in the UK with their masters. While they were in Britain they were just domestic servants and could leave their master at any time, but in the West Indies they remained enslaved, so if ever they returned they went back into slavery. The most notable person who did this in the UK was Mary Prince, who left her owner in 1828 and wrote *The West Indian Slave*, published in 1831, which became a major document in the campaign for the abolition of slavery.

The Industrial Revolution
There has been a mill at Moseley for centuries. The original mill was built in 1542, and from 1755 it was leased by Mathew Boulton, who converted the mill for making buttons and metal rolling. He was one of the pioneers for the Industrial Revolution and a member of the Lunar Society for scientific experimentation, which debated scientific discoveries on the eve of a full moon to make travelling by coach easier. The building shown on the next page dates from 1771 and was used as a mill up until 1919. Restored in 1969, it has become a tourist attraction. It is unclear if any items made at the mill by Boulton were used in slavery, but the mill was definitely part of Boulton's rise in and his involvement in the Industrial Revolution, which was partly funded through the ability to supply metal items and steam engines for use on the plantations that employed enslaved labour.

The Black Country (Dudley, Sandwell, Walsall and Wolverhampton) was one of the main areas that grew during the Industrial Revolution. The coal supplies made it a natural draw for ironworks and the addition of canals made moving raw materials cheaper and quicker.

Sarehole Mill, Moseley, c. 1910.

The soot from the factories gave the region its name, the Black Country, as illustrated by this c. 1900 postcard.

Even though little evidence for any local business involvement in slavery exists today, the area would have been at the forefront of manufacturing items for use in enslavement and as trading goods for captive Africans.

Banks and Financial Institutions

To allow the economy to grow, new financial services were required. This included a banking system that would lend funds and insurance to minimise the losses of any failed business venture. Banks and insurance companies were at the heart of the developing Empire, and of the slave trade. Bills of credit became core to the slave trade, while maritime insurance, centred around Lloyd's of London, underwrote the risk of moving the human cargo across the Atlantic.

Many of the financial institutions based in London have their roots in the slave trade. As they grew, many modern banks and insurance companies have incorporated smaller older businesses, so the direct connection to enslavement is easily lost. For example, Heywood's Bank was formed by a Liverpool slave trader and became part of Barclay's Bank.

The Bank of England, set up in 1694, underpinned commercial credit, and its members were often men made wealthy through the slave trade. The Bank of England also enabled wars and military action to be financed, securing British interests overseas. This often meant protecting the Caribbean Islands, which employed enslaved labour, and the slave trade itself.

The Royal Exchange and the Bank of England, London, 1910.

Canary Wharf, London, 2008.

The Guildhall

This magnificent building is an architectural gem on a tour of London. However, the façade hides the fact that the Guildhall was where fifteen Lord Mayors of London, twenty-five sheriffs and thirty-eight aldermen of the City of London met between 1660 and 1690. All were shareholders in the Royal African Company, which owned a monopoly in the British slave trade. These connections were not short lived, as throughout the eighteenth and early nineteenth century many people connected with the Guildhall were also involved in slavery. The most notable was William Beckford Senior (1709–1770), for whom there is a statue in the Guildhall. He owned over 20,000 acres of plantations in Jamaica and was Lord Mayor of London twice and MP for the City of London. It was also in the Guildhall that the case of the massacre aboard the slave ship *Zong* was heard in 1783.

Entrance to the Guildhall,
Gresham Street, London, 2008.

Docks and Ports

The large docks in Bristol and Liverpool get all the attention when discussing slavery. However, Whitehaven, the main port in Cumbria, which grew through exporting coal and iron, also benefited from the growing slave trade, with 15,000 Africans being carried in ships sailing from Whitehaven. A further 30,000 were transported in ships from Lancaster, and Glasgow and Plymouth also had a significant trade in Africans.

Historic images seem to capture the majestic nature of sailing ships and give a sense of adventure for the crew onboard. The truth was rather different. Bristol's position on the River Avon and its route into the Severn Estuary meant that it developed as a major trading port; indeed, becoming the second largest in England after London. Its vast wealth was made when it became the prime British port for slave trading, peaking between 1730 and 1745. From the 1650s its trade with the Caribbean had been flourishing, but it was after the Royal African Company, based in London, lost its monopoly on slave trading in 1698 that Bristol started to get involved in the slave trade. Ships owned by the Bristol-based Society of Merchant Venturers, who had lobbied against the Royal African Company's monopoly, started to trade in slaves, and the first official Bristolian slave ship, *The Beginning*, thus departed to collect a cargo of enslaved Africans. Some estimate that a fifth of all Africans carried on British slave ships were carried aboard Bristol-based ships.

Today, the docks have been reclaimed and are part of a vibrant revival of Bristol, now being home to shops, cafés, bars, restaurants and tourist attractions like the SS *Great Britain*. Many people who visit the area are still unaware that this was once the hub of the British slave trade.

Docks and wharfs were notorious hang-out spots for criminals, and theft of cargo was commonplace. At the same time, delays in unloading the ships could be costly. Robert Milligan found this unacceptable and wanted to have more control over the goods, mostly sugar, which he and other businessmen were importing from the West Indies. He headed a group of powerful businessmen who developed the West India Docks, creating a monopoly on the import of sugar, rum and coffee from the West Indies into London for twenty-one years.

The Docks' foundation stone was laid in July 1800, when Milligan was Deputy Chairman of the West India Dock Company. Those attending read as a who's who of politics of the day: the stone was laid by Lord Chancellor Lord Loughborough and Prime Minister William Pitt the Younger, as well as company Chairman George Hibbert. The Docks opened in August 1802 and Milligan thenceforth served as Chairman of the company.

Whitehaven Dock,
Cumbria, 1840.

Bristol Docks, *c.* 1900.

Bristol Dock from
Cabot's Tower, 2007.

West India Dock, London, published 1823.

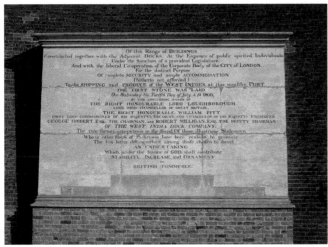

The foundation stone recording the setting up of the West India Docks, London, photographed in 2010.

Museum of London Docklands, 2008.

Like many docks, the West India Dock went through a period of decline. Regeneration has seen the buildings open up as apartments and businesses, while the old sugar warehouse has been reformed into the Museum of London Docklands. In 2007, the permanent gallery 'Sugar and Slavery' opened to record the involvement of the dockyard in the wider story of enslavement.

The Albert Docks were opened in 1846, and were made without using timber, so were the first non-combustible docks in Britain. Though constructed post-slavery in the British colonies, the warehouses stored items produced by enslaved labour in other countries, such as sugar from Cuba. The docks show a legacy of the British slave trade as the construction of such an innovative dock was only possible because of the wealth built up in Liverpool when the city was heavily involved in the slave trade. Inside Liverpool's town hall there are carvings of African heads and elephants, which reference how the town made its wealth through Africa. Between 1787 and 1807, all of the town's mayors were involved in the slave trade.

Once a major port in the slave trade and receiving cargoes of produce farmed and prepared by enslaved labour, the Liverpool Docks went into a period of decline. In recent years they have undergone major regeneration, including the development of several museums. One of these is the International Slavery Museum, which opened in 2007 as part of the commemorations of the bicentenary of the abolition of the British slave trade. The museum is now a lobbying agency to record all past and modern forms of slavery.

The *Mayflower*

In 1620, persecuted English Puritans set sail on the *Mayflower*. They boarded their ship in the Barbican, Plymouth, having made the choice to go to the New World for a new life. The actions of this group of white Europeans is commemorated by the memorial of the Mayflower Steps at, or near, to the place they boarded their ship. Alongside this memorial are plaques recognising this as the stepping stone for Europeans to go and settle in Newfoundland, Roanoke (in the USA), New Zealand and Australia. However, in 1562, John Hawkins set sail from nearly the exact spot as the *Mayflower* and became the leader of the first English expedition to buy captured Africans in Africa and transport them to the New World to be sold as enslaved labour, taking part in the now infamous triangular trade. It is ironic that there is no monument, no recognition, of this dubious English first.

This tranquil and well-kept tourist attraction hides the reality that this was the starting point of the first English journey along the route of the infamous slavery Triangular Trade by John Hawkins.

Entrance to the International Slavery Museum, Albert Docks, Liverpool, 2007.

Above: Albert Docks, 1846.

Left: Replica of the slave ship *Amistad* in Albert Docks, Liverpool, 2007.

Looking out to sea through the Mayflower Memorial at the Barbican, Plymouth, 2018.

Pleasure crafts and fishing vessels in Sutton Harbour, looking towards the Barbican, 2018.

Small Towns and Slavery

It wasn't just the large cities that had trading connections with the slave trade, or with supplying the plantation owners with their goods and importing produce farmed by enslaved labour. Small towns better known today for fishing and/or tourism were an integral part of the commercial triangle with Africa and the Americas. Ships loaded with cargo at Bideford Quay (shown below) serviced plantations in Carolina and Virginia, returning with tobacco. Some of the local merchants were also encouraged to try their hand with slave trading from Africa due to the potential profits it could bring, usually linking with Bristol merchants.

The Navy

The in many ways contradictory role of the Royal Navy in the nineteenth century regarding the transatlantic slave trade is well illustrated by the Navy base at Devonport Dockyard, Plymouth. Here the Royal Navy built ships both in their own dock and in private docks that were used both to suppress the slave trade post its abolition in 1807, but also to maintain status quo and to prevent uprisings in the British territory that still employed slaves until the 1834 Emancipation Act. As examples, the following ships launched in the present boundary of Plymouth can be used:

- HMS *Racehorse*, launched in 1830. This eighteen-gun sloop was built at the Royal Naval Devonport Dockyard. She sailed to the West Indies and while there helped end an insurrection of enslaved workers in Jamaica in 1831/32 (known as the Baptist Wars led by Sam Sharpe – now a national hero in Jamaica), and restored order in Montego Bay.
- HMS *Derwent*, launched in 1807. This eighteen-gun sloop-brig was built in the private yard of Isaac Blackburne at Turnchapel. She was one of the first two Navy ships to patrol African Coast to interrupt the slave trade from 1808 to 1810.

Bideford, Devon, 1907.

Bideford Quay, Devon, *c.* 1910.

Devonport Royal Naval Dockyard, *c.* 1910.

HMS *Rifleman* chasing down a Brazilian slaver, 1850. This was one of many images that appeared in the *Illustrated London News* during the Victorian era, depicting Royal Navy ships chasing down and capturing slave ships.

The docks where these ships were built remain today, albeit in heavily modified and extended versions, and maintain the present Navy. Plymouth in some ways continues the ethos of the anti-slavery patrols carried out in the nineteenth century with humanitarian efforts led by the Amphibious Assault Team based there. The Royal Navy also offers support in trying to deter human traffickers.

Railways

When compensation was paid to free the enslaved in 1834, a lot of this money did not go to plantation owners, but to those in Britain that had provided banking services and loans, and who were owed money by the previous slave owners. As many of those who had received this compensation had only invested money into the slavery business for profit, once their investment was returned they looked for new opportunities. Infrastructure offered the promise of a quick profit, so some of their money was then invested in programmes such as the development of railways and canals. Others who had benefitted from owning slaves and had made their wealth from their plantations also looked for the same investment opportunities. It is hard to follow the money, but there is no coincidence that some of these developments began in the late 1830s, just after emancipation.

In Bristol in 1832, the inaugural meeting of the Great Western Railway Company was held in the Merchants' Hall. The railway received financial support from members of the Merchant Venturers and Temple Meads station was opened in 1840 as the western end of the Great Western Railway, linking the city to London. The station was designed by Isambard Kingdom Brunel and was soon being used by the Bristol & Exeter Railway, the Bristol & Gloucester Railway, the Bristol Harbour Railway and the Bristol & South Wales Union Railway. These new railway companies had sought funding and some of the money invested was the compensation payments to the slave owners. Even though the station was expanded several times, it still stands as a legacy to those who made profits from slavery and how this money was used in the development of infrastructure post-emancipation.

Railways in the 1830 Series, showing the Railway Office in Liverpool, postmarked 1905.

Temple Meads railway station, Bristol, 1906.

Chapter 5

Collectables

The British are a nation of collectors and three of the main items collected are coins (including medals and tokens), stamps and postcards. In all three, the legacy of slavery and emancipation can be found. Though the connections might not be that clear, especially when considering postcards, stamps, coins and tokens at least were specifically issued as commemorative items, such as the set of six stamps issued to mark the bicentenary of the abolition of the slave trade in 2007, showing William Wilberforce, Olaudah Equiano, Granville Sharp, Thomas Clarkson, Hannah More and Ignatius Sancho.

Tokens
Spence's Token
Thomas Spence (1750–1814) was a radical and supporter of the French Revolution. He set up a radical bookshop in London where he sold publications like Thomas Paine's *Rights of Man* (page 20) as well as his own writings. Alongside the books he started to sell tokens. One of these was the anti-slavery token shown below. It has been argued that Spence did not press the tokens himself, but rather commissioned them to be made for him. Due to sharing the same Christian name as Sir Thomas More and Thomas Paine, Thomas Spence's token is often referred to as the Three Thomas's token.

Spence's Token, 1795.

Sierra Leone Token
This token commemorates the end to the British slave trade in 1807 and was circulated in Sierra Leone from 1814. It depicts a white British man shaking hands with an African, and in the distance are a village and people dancing in celebration. The Arabic inscription translates to: 'THE SALE OF SLAVES PROHIBITED IN ENGLAND IN 1807 OF THE CHRISTIAN ERA IN THE REIGN OF SULTAN GEORGE III, VERILY WE ARE ALL

Sierra Leone Token, issued in 1814.

BROTHERS.' It has been suggested that these tokens were made in Birmingham at the Soho mint by James Watt Junior.

'Am I Not a Woman and a Sister' Token

Even though this is an American token issued in 1838, it made use of the kneeling woman image created for the anti-slavery women's groups in Britain. The token was struck by Gibbs, Gardner & Company of Belleville, New Jersey, in 1837 during the Financial Panic of 1837/38. These were 'hard luck' tokens created when America was hit by a recession and merchants purchased tokens from local mints. This token primarily circulated in New York and there was an accompanying 'Am I Not a Man and a Brother' token.

'Am I Not a Woman and a Sister' Token. This example is probably a copy.

King William IV Tokens

This token depicts on one side King William IV stating 'I advocate this bill as a measure of humanity', and on the other it shows former enslaved workers dancing. The medal was made by Thomas Halliday who worked in Birmingham between 1810 and 1842. He manufactured

Token created to commemorate the 1834 Act.

King William IV Token, 1837.

tokens and medals for his own works, and that of others. He produced a second token in 1838, which marked the end of apprentice scheme and total 'Emancipation in the West Indies'. It showed an African shakings hands with a European man and listed those British white men who had been pivotal in the Act: Penn, Granville Sharp, Wilberforce, Benezet, Buxton, Brougham, Sturge and Sligo.

A second token commemorates King William IV and the major achievements of his government during his reign; namely, the Reform Act of 1832 and the abolition of slavery in 1834. The coin notes the major dates in King William IV's life and the date of his death, 20 June 1837.

Stamps
An exhibition, using the collection of the author, was part of a year-long programme to mark the centenary of the accession of George V – the philatelist king – which used a wide range of stamps to create exhibitions throughout the UK. This exhibition looked at the wide range of postage stamps produced since 1888 that commemorated the end of slavery throughout the world, but mostly in the Caribbean and South America. Many of these stamps are held in museum and archive collections.

Above and below: Exhibition of stamps in Museum of London Docklands, 2010.

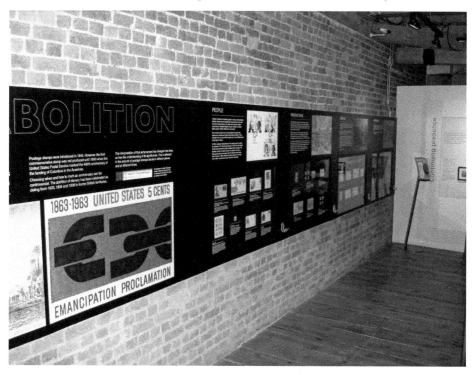

Chapter 6

Racism

In a publication like this, a sensitive subject like racism cannot be covered with the completeness or depth that it deserves. However, it cannot be ignored either. While buildings and statues give a tangible link to enslavement and emancipation, it is often the intangibles that are harder to understand, but which have the greater impact. Racism is such an integral part of the story of slavery and is still all around us, whether we see and feel it or not. When it becomes visible or audible through racist graffiti, racist language and racist chanting, it becomes a very vocal and very visual legacy of slavery.

During slavery, Africans were not seen as equal to the white European and became little more than a trade item, on the same level as animals. Enslaved workers became categorised by their parentage, with often their description being linked to how much of their ancestry was white. The whole fight for emancipation was also viewed as one of inequality, with the enslaved begging for their freedom, and the white masters giving it to them. Nothing was further from the truth and a major incentive for the end of slavery was not the moral argument, but the financial cost to the government and local communities in the West Indies gleaned from civil disobedience and rebellion, with the enslaved fighting for their freedom.

When slavery ended, racism didn't, and often this prejudice was used as a means to legally justify divisions and inequality. The racism created by slavery and considering darker skin inferior was reinforced by the end of the nineteenth century by scientific racism, which tried to legitimise the difference between white and black populations through differences in intelligence and physical capabilities.

Britain's Black Presence
There is a perception that Britain only gained a black presence with the arrival of people from the West Indies in the 1950s. However, modern genetics studies not only make a farce of racism, but also show how long there has been a black population in Britain. We all originate from Africa and have ancestors who would have been black. For some, this inconvenient truth was hidden by the fact that the migration from Africa was so long ago. However, a report in 2018 announced that in England, DNA from the Cheddar Man, dating back 10,000 years, strongly suggested he had dark skin.

Probably the earliest written records of a black presence date to the third century when 500 Moors (North Africans) were stationed at Hadrian's Wall. Later, as Britain's naval might grew and trading aspirations developed Britain into the world's largest empire, ports like those in Liverpool, Bristol and London gained a large black presence, mostly comprising sailors and crew members who settled on our shores. Some would have been freed enslaved workers, or the descendants of enslaved Africans. There would have been some discrimination based on colour and class, but nowhere near the racism that really appeared at the end of the nineteenth century and in the beginning of the twentieth.

The Windrush Generation

Many people think that multicultural Britain started after the Second World War and was symbolised by the arrival of SS *Windrush* from the Caribbean. Television programmes like *Who Do You Think You Are?* highlight the importance of the *Windrush* as those celebrities with African heritage, like Ainsley Harriott and Colin Jackson, trace their connections back to the Caribbean through family members immigrating to Britain in the 1950s and '60s.

However, this is far from the truth. In 1772, it was estimated that there was between 10,000 and 15,000 black people living in Britain, and that 1 per cent of the population of London was black. This population was boosted by an influx of black loyalists in the 1780s, who were welcomed following the loss of America following the War of Independence. In 1787, encouraged by the Committee for the Relief of the Black Poor, 4,000 black Londoners were aided in emigrating to Sierra Leone in West Africa, founding the first British colony on the continent. The Windrush Generation, however, did see the fastest and biggest increase in the number of black people living in Britain. By 1950, there were around 20,000 black people living in Britain, and by 1961 it was nearly over 190,000. By the time the 2011 census was taken, numbers had increased to around 1.9 million.

The Windrush Generation arrived in Britain at a time when it was still rebuilding from the devastation of the Second World War. Even though the labour force was welcomed, they entered a Britain that in part was racist and lacking tolerance. Many didn't mind if the recently arrived immigrants did the low level and dirty jobs that the existing British population didn't want to do, but there were major concerns on how they could assimilate into society and how it would affect the accepted social norms of the day.

Minstrel Shows and Blackface

An obvious example of persisting racism can be found in *The Black and White Minstrel Show*, which continued on television until the 1970s. Minstrel shows started off on the beaches in Victorian Britain to entertain the growing day-tripper and holidaying population. This was extended to the end of the pier shows. The Clacton-on-Sea Pier postcard on page 87 appears to depict a quiet day at the beach, and it is not until you look closer that you notice the show being performed on the pier. The White Coon show, set up in 1899, featured Will C. Pepper's white minstrel performers, who 'blacked up' their faces. These shows were popular and existed until the 1970s. Clarkson Rose, in his book *Beside the Seaside* (1960), recalls how he watched performers blacking up on the beach before performing, and that this was one of the reasons he wanted a life on the stage. His book offers no excuses or explanations of the Black Minstrel phenomenon.

On page 87 is a picture of the crew of HMS *Chester* are in fancy dress. On the front row, one is dressed as Kaiser Bill, while another is 'Old Bill', a cartoon character created during the First World War. However, as was common throughout much of the twentieth century, one of the men has 'blacked up', and can be seen standing behind the seated men. This was commonly deemed acceptable until about the 1980s, when the racist overtones of blackface became viewed as unacceptable.

Many would have thought that 'blacking up', or putting on blackface, for entertainment was a thing of the past. Unhappily, it is not a phenomenon consigned to history. Not all people understand the connotations, and no matter whether they mean offence, or are looking for a satirical approach, the outcome is the same – shock. In May 2018, the Oratory School in Oxfordshire School allowed an informal school photograph of pupils dressed in fancy dress. Teachers were horrified when a group of sixth formers created a tableau of a slave gang, with the white boys dressed as black enslaved workers, and the black pupils dressed as their white slave owners. The school refused their inclusion in the formal picture but the pupils posted an informal one on social media. The spokesperson stated that the school was 'extremely

Clacton-on-Sea
Pier Pavilion,
c. 1910.

HMS *Chester*
concert party,
c. 1916.

Liverpool
Pageant, *c.* 1910.

shocked and saddened' and apologised 'unreservedly for the offence caused', stating that: 'The Oratory School unequivocally condemns racist imagery of any sort: we are a diverse and inclusive community,' and 'We will strengthen our tutorial programme to ensure that it is understood by all our pupils that such representations are utterly unacceptable.'

On the other hand, the image of the Liverpool Pageant in *c.* 1910 avoids creating racist stereotypes by at least using black people to represent the enslaved, rather than white people with black makeup. However, the card still leaves the modern viewer feeling uncomfortable with the portrayal, especially as it was in a city that benefitted greatly from the slave trade.

Golliwogs

The Golliwog (later to be just called Golly) is the formalisation of a traditional rag doll hailing from the USA in the nineteenth century. Author Florence Kate Upton created the Golliwog to appear in her children's books. Born in the USA in 1873, she moved to England aged fourteen and first included the character in her children's books in 1895, initially as the villain and then as a friendly character, which she attributed with 'a kind face'. Toy companies and publishers then created products for children that included the Golliwog, and these were at their height in the 1960s and 1970s, which coincided with the resurgence of blackface minstrels, such as in the television show *The Black and White Minstrels*, mentioned previously. To try and deflect some of the negative connotations, the doll was renamed the Golly.

At the start of the twentieth century, John Robertson, grandson of the founder of James Robertson & Sons, Preserve Manufacturers, went on a trip to the USA. He saw children playing with homemade black rag dolls with exaggerated facial features and for some reason he felt that the image would make an ideal mascot. It first appeared in company literature in 1910, and from 1928 the company became associated with their Golly enamelled badges. Soon, special editions were produced for royal events, the first being for King George VI's coronation in 1937. Along with badges, there was a wide range of products such as dolls, ceramics, games for children and even Golly clothing. Tokens were produced so they could be collected and swapped for a badge.

By the late 1970s and early 1980s, the image was no longer seen as acceptable. For example, Black Jacks, the liquorice-flavoured sweet, used the face of a Golliwog on the wrapper until 1983, when it was replaced by a pirate, but surprisingly, while other items were stopped, Robertson Preserves continued to produce their badges until 2001, by which time over 20 million had been

Above: A 1930s postcard produced by Bamforth & Co. in Yorkshire.

Left: Undated postcard.

Robertson Gollies playing sports.

Robertson Gollies playing musical instruments.

sent out. The company claim that they did not retire the Golly because of political correctness, but because of a rebranding strategy, stating: 'We are retiring Golly because we found families with kids no longer necessarily knew about him. We are not bowing to political correctness, but like with any great make, we have to move with the times'. The badges are now collector's items and are available for purchase on online auction sites.

Racism Today
Even though great steps have been taken to reduce racism, it is still part of British life. Campaigns like 'Let's Kick Racism Out of Football' illustrate that racist chants, even though less common, can still sometimes be heard.

Chapter 7

The United Kingdom Overseas Territories

Many people either don't know or forget that Britain still has territories that they have jurisdiction and sovereignty over. Of the fourteen United Kingdom Overseas Territories (UKOT), five are Caribbean islands – Anguilla, British Virgin Islands, Cayman Islands, Montserrat and the Turks and Caicos Islands – and, along with Bermuda and Saint Helena, these seven all have remaining evidence that these were islands heavily connected with the slave trade or the fight against it. Therefore, while the British Government has some limited legal responsibility, it definitely has a moral responsibility for safeguarding these important sites in the UKOT. Unfortunately, development in these islands, often to create facilities for tourists, is removing these tangible links to the islands' slave heritage. For example, the new airport runway in St Helena was built over the site where thousands of freed Africans were buried after being saved from slave ships post 1808, but who later died on the island, weakened as they were by their treatment during their capture or onboard the ship.

Below are a few examples of the history and continued remembrances of the slave trade on a selection of these islands.

Anguilla
In 1819, there were 360 Europeans, 320 free Africans and 2,451 slaves living on Anguilla. A full-blown plantation economy was not possible on the island due to its poor soil and climate, and even though a few small sugar and cotton plantations did exist, they struggled, so the island developed a salt industry to utilise the same conditions, producing salt from sea water in large ponds. Koal Keel was built using enslaved workers in the 1700s for a Dutch family from St Maarten, and operated as a sugar and cotton plantation before being

Koal Keel, Anguilla, 2006.

abandoned. It was later purchased by the descendants of some of those who had been enslaved on the plantation and recently has been home to a bake-house and restaurant.

Bermuda
The Royal Navy Dockyards was the base for the North America and West Indies Station from 1818. The original buildings were constructed using free or enslaved labour, who were also used in the building and repairing of the ships. Some of the free men were freed Africans from slave ships captured after 1807. Ships from here not only helped to capture slave ships after the 1807 Abolition of the Slave Trade Act, but also helped enforce the political and economic structure that required the use of enslaved labour. The Navy closed most of the Dockyard in 1958 and it was redeveloped as a major tourist attraction, and includes the Bermuda Maritime Museum.

The British Virgin Islands
The idealised view of the Caribbean islands, comprising blue waters and beaches, hides their origins as islands that would have been developed by enslaved labour. Tourists seem to forget this as they move from one beach to another. However, some locals try to remind themselves and the visitors of their past, sometimes through murals, as shown below.

Right: Royal Navy Dockyard, Bermuda, 2001.

Below left and right: Murals in the British Virgin Islands, 2003.

Even though the copper mine at Virgin Gorda was not constructed until 1837, it would have used labour that had been born as enslaved workers, who would have used skills learned during their enslavement. When operational it employed thirty-six Cornish miners and around 140 British Virgin Islands workmen. The ore was shipped to Wales (page 58), with returning ships carrying wood to be used for construction and coal to power the steam engine serving the mine.

The Cayman Islands
The Plantation House, Pedro St James, was constructed in 1780 as the home of William Eden. However, it is more famous as the location where the first elected parliament of the Cayman Islands met and as the location where, in 1835, the Slavery Abolition Act was read – a year later than everywhere else because the island was governed by Jamaica and they had to wait until Governor Sligo could journey from Jamaica to read out the Act. The house fell into disrepair, but after reconstruction in 1996 it is now a tourist attraction.

Montserrat
Montserrat's capital would have originally been built using the labour of enslaved workers. Up until the 1990s, visitors and residents could still walk down these streets, viewing some of these historic buildings. However, the volcanic eruptions of 1995 and 1997 saw Plymouth covered in volcanic ash and the historic centre put out of bounds. In one action, Mother Nature removed a lasting legacy of Montserrat by burying not only Plymouth, but also some of the former plantation sites. One of the effects was to displace a high percentage of the

Copper mine ruins, Virgin Gorda, British Virgin Islands, 2003.

Plantation House, Pedro St James, Grand Cayman, 2007.

Parliament Street, Plymouth, Montserrat, *c.* 1910.

Looking towards Plymouth, Montserrat, in 2015, showing the devastation and scarring almost a decade after the eruption.

Montserrat population around the world, especially to England, who brought with them their legacy of the period of enslavement.

The Endangered Archive Programme, run by the British Library, enabled archives in some of the UKOTs to run projects to digitise some of their remaining archives. Even though these projects were mainly aimed at assessing the present condition of all the archival material held in the countries involved, some material related to enslavement was uncovered. The hope is that these projects will lead to the better preservation of the archives and to the release of information contained within the records.

Turks and Caicos Islands

The wreck of the *Troubadour* (extensively researched between 2000 and 2008, the year it was announced the wreck had been discovered and identified) illustrates that there is still a lot of slavery heritage to be discovered. Wrecked in 1841, all the Africans aboard survived, and as this was a British territory, they were freed. Most of them stayed in this small chain of islands to work in the salt industry, increasing the population by around 7 per cent as a result. The settlements of East Harbour on South Caicos and Bambara on Middle Caicos grew most likely because of their presence. This is a story of the triangular trade and also of emancipation and freedom because they did not reach the slave markets of Cuba.

The country also contains several buildings linked to the period of enslavement. There is Cheshire Hall Plantation (see page 6) and the parish church of St Thomas, which was built in the early 1820s using enslaved labour supplied by Wade Stubbs, the largest slave owner on the Turks and Caicos Islands and who had owned Cheshire Hall.

Above left: A review of some of the archives in Montserrat, 2015.

Above right: A cathead beam from the slave ship *Troubadour*, found during the archaeological search off East Caicos in 2006.

Below: St Thomas's Church, Turks and Caicos Islands, 2006.

Acknowledgements

I would like to thank my wife, Vicky, and son, Fred, for their support during the production of this publication, and my parents, Liz and Paul Sadler, who gave me my passion for history. I would also like to than the many researchers who have uncovered the stories of the legacy of slavery in the UK. All of the historic images used in this publication are from the archive of Sands of Time Consultancy and all modern photographs were taken by the author.

Bibliography

Ashley, Mike, *Taking Liberties: The Struggle for Britain's Freedoms and Rights* (London: British Library, 2008).

Coules, Victoria, *The Trade. Bristol and the Transatlantic Slave Trade* (Edinburgh: Birlinn, 2007).

Curtin, Philip D., *The Rise and Fall of The Plantation Complex* (Cambridge: Cambridge University Press, 1998).

Eickelmann, Christine and David Small, *Pero: The Life of a Slave in Eighteenth Century Bristol*, (Bristol: Redcliffe Press, 2004).

Equiano, Olaudah, *The Interesting Narrative of the Life of Olaudah Equiano: or Gustavus Vassa, the African* (London: 1789).

Evans, Chris, *Slave Wales: The Welsh and Atlantic Slavery, 1660–1850* (Cardiff: University of Wales Press 2010).

Everett, Susanne, *History of Slavery: An Illustrated History of the Monstrous Evil* (New Jersey: Chartwell Books Inc, 2006).

Ferguson, Moira, *The History of Mary Prince, a West Indian Slave* (Michigan: University of Michigan Press, 1996)

Hague, William, *William Wilberforce: The Life of the Great Anti-Slave Trade Campaigner* (London: Harper Collins Publishers, 2007).

Hochschild, Adam, *Bury The Chains: The British Struggle to Abolish Slavery* (London: Macmillan, 2005).

Kalman, Bobbie, *Life on a Plantation* (Oxford: Crabtree Publishing, 1997).

Klein, Herbert S., *The Atlantic Slave Trade* (Cambridge: Cambridge University Press, 1999).

Martin, S. I., *Britain's Slave Trade* (London: Macmillan Publishers, 1999).

McEvedy, Colin, *The Penguin Atlas of African History* (London: Penguin, 1995).

Monaghan, Tom, *The Slave Trade* (London: Evans Brothers Limited, 2002).

Parekh, Bhikhu, *The Future of Multi-Ethnic Britain* (London: Profile Books, 2000).

Rattansi, Ali, *Racism: A Very Short Introduction* (Oxford University Press: 2007).

Reddie, Richard S., *Abolition! The Struggle to Abolish Slavery in the British Colonies* (Oxford: Lion Hudson, 2007).

St Clair, William, *The Grand Slave Emporium: Cape Coast Castle and the British Slave Trade* (London: Profile Books, 2007).

Thomas, Hugh, *The Slave Trade: The Story of the Atlantic Slave Trade 1440–1870* (New York: Simon & Schuster, 1999).

Walvin, James, *Questioning Slavery* (Jamaica: Ian Randle Publishers, 1997).

Walvin, James, *The Slave Trade* (Stroud: Sutton Publishing Limited, 1999).

Ward, W. E. F., *The Royal Navy and the Slavers: The Suppression of the Atlantic Slave Trade* (New York: Pantheon Books, 1968).